ue

Economic Analysis for International Trade Negotiations

This book is dedicated to

Don and Audrey Gaisford

and

Jill and Anna Hobbs

Economic Analysis for International Trade Negotiations

The WTO and Agricultural Trade

James D. Gaisford
Associate Professor of Economics, University of Calgary, Canada

William A. Kerr
Van Vliet Professor, University of Saskatchewan, Canada

Edward Elgar
Cheltenham, UK • Northampton, MA, USA

Published by
Edward Elgar Publishing Limited
Glensanda House
Montpellier Parade
Cheltenham
Glos GL50 1UA
UK

Edward Elgar Publishing, Inc.
136 West Street
Suite 202
Northampton
Massachusetts 01060
USA

A catalogue record for this book
is available from the British Library

Library of Congress Cataloguing in Publication Data

Gaisford, James D.
    Economic analysis for international trade negotiations : the WTO and agricultural trade / James D. Gaisford, William A. Kerr.
    Includes bibliographical references and index.
    1. World Trade Organization. 2. Produce trade–Government policy–International cooperation. 3. Tariff on farm produce. I. Kerr, William A., 1947–II. Title.

HF 1385 .G35 2000
382'.41–dc21

00–046657

ISBN 1 84064 535 0

Printed and bound in Great Britain by MPG Books Ltd, Bodmin, Cornwall

Contents

Figures

Tables

Preface

Trade negotiations are complex interactive processes that bring a combination of existing trade law, the pleadings of special interests and economic theory together in the give and take of compromise, bluff and strategic alliances. Governments often seek the advice of a wide spectrum of the community when establishing their opening positions at trade negotiations, when establishing their negotiating priorities and as negotiations progress. Successful trade negotiations will lead to changes in the *rules of trade*. Changes in the rules of trade will, first and foremost, have economic effects. Thus it is important to be able to assess the economic ramifications of proposed changes to trade law, of changes in negotiating strategies and of any new set of agreed rules. Being able to undertake these assessments is important for firms that engage in international commercial transactions, for firms that operate in import-competing industries, for government departments that are not directly responsible for trade negotiations, for members of the broad civil society, for students interested in the international economy as well as for those directly involved in trade negotiations.

Economic analysis of existing trade law can illuminate weaknesses and indicate possible improvements. It can be used to assess the impact of changes to trade rules on firms, employment, government finances, consumers and society's welfare. It can help identify those who may have a vested interest in protectionism or who can be expected to resist change. It can also help identify those who may be natural allies, both domestic and foreign, in trade negotiations. Sound economic reasoning can be used to debunk naïve beliefs about the effects of changing trade regimes or more purposeful attempts to mislead. Without a solid grounding in economic theory, making arguments regarding trade policy leaves one vulnerable to criticisms that are difficult to refute.

Our many years of teaching international trade combined with providing advice on trade policy to private industry, governments and international organizations made it clear that what is most often taught in university economics curricula does not stress that which is useful for conducting

xi

economic analysis pertaining to trade negotiations. Further, those charged with conducting trade analysis in both the public and private sectors may not have a strong grounding in economics – their backgrounds often being in such diverse academic disciplines as international relations, international business, political science, history, engineering and law.

While the economic approach used in this book is not particularly new – although the applications often are – its use is widely scattered in the literature. This book carefully builds the foundations of economic analysis useful in trade negotiations before going on to examine the important issues that are likely to be the subject of current and future negotiations. Further, while many of the issues discussed in the book have been analysed for previous trade negotiation sessions, a number of new and complex issues have arisen since the last major set of negotiations, the Uruguay Round of the General Agreement on Tariffs and Trade, which ended in 1994. These new issues are discussed at length and hence the book has considerable material that is not found elsewhere. The decision to use agricultural issues as a focus for the book was made for three reasons. First, the range of issues found in agriculture encompasses almost all of the issues found in other sectors, as well as many that are unique. Thus the analytical method is applied to a broad spectrum of issues which can easily be transferred to other sectors. Second, the issues in agriculture, particularly the new issues, are extremely complex and thus give the method of analysis developed in the theory section a good test. Third, agricultural trade negotiations have in the past been some of the most difficult and acrimonious. This is a trend that seems set to continue. Difficult negotiations in agriculture have the potential to threaten the very existence of the international institutions that regulate international trade.

The book attempts to be accessible to all those who have a solid basic grasp of economic principles. Academic economists and others well versed in economic theory may wish to skip some of the early material and move directly to the analysis of current topics.

Much of this material was developed formally for short courses presented to members of the Polish government. We would like to thank both Simon Davies of the Scottish Agricultural College and Michael Green of the UK Department for International Development for providing us with the opportunities to present the material formally to those directly involved in the development of trade policy. We thank the Polish officials who attended our sessions and who in turn gave us many insights, and also our students at the Universities of Calgary and Saskatchewan, who also unknowingly gave us feedback on the material.

We would like to thank the staff at Edward Elgar for their support of this project. Finally, we would like to thank Pam, Daniel, Brian, Megan and Jill, in short our families, for putting up with the long absences in front of computer screens that inevitably accompany the writing of a book.

James D. Gaisford, Calgary and William A. Kerr, Saskatoon, Canada
October 2000.

1. Introduction to the issues

1.1 GROWTH AND IMPORTANCE OF TRADE IN FOOD AND AGRICULTURAL COMMODITIES

The continued expansion of international trade in agricultural products through the early part of the 21st century is crucial for maintaining a reasonable balance between the global demand for food and its supply. Although estimates differ, there is general agreement that the growth of population, and hence demand for food, will outstrip the ability to increase food production in many developing countries (Schieb, 1999). Given current population trends, food production worldwide will have to double by 2025. The rate of population growth is, however, slowing. Projections suggest that the growth in the production of agricultural products will exceed the growth in demand over the period 2010–2020, even accounting for increased consumption as incomes rise. Currently, most agricultural surpluses arise in rich developed countries. To maintain existing diets and to have a moderate improvement in nutritional levels will require that developing countries import increasing quantities of food. It should also be remembered that 830 million people do not currently get enough to eat. If they and their children are to be adequately fed over the next 25 years, much of the additional food will have to come from foreign sources. By 2020, grain imports by developing countries could be as high as 220 million tonnes (Schieb, 1999). This volume of imports is in excess of twice the 1995 levels.

Over the period 1998–2007, all the major crop and livestock commodities are projected to have increases in traded volumes. Wheat trade is expected to increase by 23 per cent over the period, rice 20 per cent, maize 30 per cent, barley 9 per cent and sorghum 33 per cent. In oilseeds, soybean trade is projected to increase 12 per cent, soy meal 27 per cent, soy oil 32 per cent, rapeseed 34 per cent, canola meal 23 per cent, rape oil 15 per cent, sunflower seeds 20 per cent, sunflower meal 32 per cent, sunflower oil 46 per cent and palm oil 23 per cent. Sugar exports are expected to increase by 15 per cent. For meats, beef exports will rise by 34 per cent, pork by 29 per cent and poultry meat by 32 per cent. Trade in the various components of the dairy complex is also expected to show moderate growth: butter 3 per cent, non-fat dry milk 9 per cent, whole milk powder 9 per cent, with cheese being an exception at 24 per cent projected growth (FAPRI, 1998)

Dealing with the large expected increase in the volume of world trade in agricultural commodities in two decades will represent a significant challenge for agribusiness and other firms involved in the logistics and organization of trade in agricultural products. Much of the increase will be in higher value products that require more specialized handling, warehousing and transportation equipment than commodities such as grains and oilseeds. A considerable portion of the increased trade in meat products will be frozen or fresh (chilled). Firms engaged in the international trade in meat products will need complex cold chain logistics. In many parts of the world, consumer expectations regarding the quality and safety of their food are rising. As the trade in food moves into an era of higher technology, considerable investment will be required. This investment must be forward looking if the expected growth in trade is to be met. The investments required to accommodate the projected volumes of trade in commodities will also be very large. These types of facilities tend to be capital intensive and have a long life – port facilities, improvements to transportation infrastructure, storage facilities and so on. A relatively stable international business environment will be required to induce the commitment to the types of long-term investment required for a major expansion of facilities to support the expected increases in agrifood trade.

The business environment that characterizes agriculture is, however, far from stable. The vicissitudes of weather, disease, pests and predators affect output. Prices tend to be volatile. A high degree of product substitutability means that problems in one sector often spill over into another. Government policies, while well intentioned, often give inappropriate signals and make agribusiness investments vulnerable to changes in government policy or governmental fiscal difficulties.

While investing in agriculture is inherently risky, investing in projects tied to agricultural trade is even more risky. This is because the international rules of trade in agricultural commodities have remained largely outside the set of rules governing international trade since new international institutions were set up at the end of the Second World War.

In the first half of the 20th century there were no international rules for trade. Each country negotiated bilateral agreements with its trading partners. The gold standard provided an implicit and automatic system of international currency management. There was no mechanism to transfer resources to less well-off nations and economic (and political) instability was endemic in the poor areas of the globe that were not colonies. While an attempt to establish an international system for solving political disputes between nations had been made at the end of the First World War through the establishment of the League of Nations, the weakness in its organizational structure and the failure of the United States to become a member severely limited its effectiveness. From the point of view of firms wishing to invest in international commercial activity, it was a very risky environment.

Firms investing in international trading activities do not like to have their export successes nullified by the capricious use of trade barriers by governments. The absence of international rules makes it easy for countries to alter their tariffs and to put in place other trade-restricting policies. Firms engaging in international commerce prefer fixed exchange rates because most international transactions have a considerable time element. Political instability in developing countries often puts foreign investments at risk. Wars, as well as having a huge human cost, are also disruptive to commercial activity.

The fragile nature of the international system came home to roost with the advent of the Great Depression. In reaction to the deepening crisis in demand and employment, countries raised trade barriers in a spate of 'beggar thy neighbour' trade wars. World trade dropped by two-thirds in less than a decade. Agricultural commodities were particularly heavily hit by tariff increases and other trade-restricting measures as countries attempted to help their farmers. The gold standard was abandoned and countries engaged in strategic devaluations. The deepening economic crisis led to loan defaults in poor countries and a general rise in instability. While the trade wars did not *cause* the Great Depression, high trade barriers and international financial instability made it both deeper and longer than it need have been. The long depression and subsequent difficulties in acquiring resources through trade (particularly in the case of Japan) led to an increase in military adventurism which the League of Nations was powerless to stop. This may have been a contributor to the outbreak of the Second World War.

At the end of the Second World War the allies, particularly the United

States and the United Kingdom, wished to establish a New World Order to ensure that the economic and political mayhem of the pre-war period would not be repeated. A new and stronger United Nations was founded to reduce the threat of war. The International Monetary Fund (IMF) was set up to manage a new fixed exchange rate regime and to prevent the strategic use of devaluations. The International Bank for Reconstruction and Development – the World Bank – was established, first to transfer resources to war-damaged economies and then to developing countries to encourage stability and growth. A broad-based International Trade Organization (ITO) was negotiated to manage international trade. These institutions were intended to be the four pillars of the New World Order and, while it was probably not their primary intent, considerably reduced the risks associated with international business.

The US Congress, however, would not pass the ITO legislation and the organization was never established. The ITO negotiations did produce the General Agreement on Tariffs and Trade (GATT); whose primary rationale was the reduction of tariffs on the trade in goods. This facet of the ITO was passed by the US Congress and became the *de facto* organization for managing international trade. The absence of a broad-based international trade body like the ITO was not particularly crucial because the major inhibitor of international trade was the extremely high tariffs which had been enacted prior to the Second World War and which remained in place. The GATT was a forum for negotiating the reduction of tariffs and had considerable success over the next decades. As tariffs came down, however, other inhibitors of trade became more important. The GATT was less suited to the task of reducing these non-tariff barriers. In addition, whereas technological changes were making trade in services increasingly important, the GATT dealt exclusively with trade in goods. Further, the proportion of goods' value comprised of intellectual property increased rapidly in the wake of the computer, biotechnological and electronic entertainment revolutions, and developed countries needed an international mechanism to protect their intellectual property rights. These deficiencies in the GATT led to the creation of a new broad-based World Trade Organization (WTO) in 1994. It was expected that it would fulfil the role devised for the ITO 50 years earlier.

While the institutions of the New World Order have not worked exactly as envisioned, they have proved remarkably durable. The GATT and its members were rolled into the WTO. The IMF's fixed exchange rate regime is long since gone but it still has an active and relatively successful role in international finance. While controversial, the World Bank remains the primary organization charged with transferring resources to developing countries. The United Nations is active in peacekeeping the world over, although it has fallen far short of removing war as a policy option. From the perspective of those engaged in international business, these organizations have greatly increased the security of investments through the reduction of both the level of trade barriers and their capricious use; brought a degree of stability to international currency markets; and reduced political instability and likely the devastation brought by war. As a result, during the last quarter of the 20th century international trade grew at a faster rate than individual national economies and was perceived as one of the engines of growth (Kerr and Perdikis, 1995).

While trade in agricultural commodities has been increasing, agribusiness firms have not enjoyed the same level of security for their investments in international activities as other firms making such investments. This is because trade in agricultural commodities has been, almost since the Agreement's inception, largely outside the GATT rules for trade. At the Uruguay Round of GATT negotiations (1986–94), a first step was taken towards the integration of agriculture into the general rules governing international trade. That process was to continue through further negotiations commencing in 2000. Given the magnitude of the investment in international trading infrastructure required to facilitate the expected increase in international agrifood trade, the new set of negotiations will be crucial. The degree of surety provided to agribusiness will factor heavily in future investment decisions.

A smoothly functioning international trade system has an important role in bringing stability to the entire system. If investments are not made in trade-enhancing infrastructure, local shortages and surpluses will determine prices to a greater degree. Price instability in agriculture means that prices cannot act efficiently in their role as the signaller for the commitment of resources to economic activity (Hobbs, Kerr and Gaisford, 1997). If farmers receive incorrect signals and act on them, even to a partial degree, the possibility of production and price cycles arises. Cyclical markets exacerbate the difficulties caused by natural phenomena such as droughts or insect infestations and generally increase the risks associated with agricultural production, with commensurate long-run effects on investment in the sector. If prices do not provide the correct signals, and farmers do not have a sound basis for resource commitment decisions, then the question remains as to the criteria on which such decisions are made. Prices play a central role in resource allocation in a market system. Given the poor performance of agricultural prices as signalling devices, it is probably not surprising that there has been, and continues to be, a large degree of government intervention in agricultural markets. Trade, through its ability to arbitrage between markets, can considerably improve the signalling function of prices. Improvements to price discovery will lead to reduced risk and hence increased production. This will assist in meeting the expected increases in global demand.

The projected increases in population in developing countries will put additional pressure on local resources, raising the probability of local crop failures. Larger populations may also lead to increased human demands for groundwater in times of drought, reducing the availability of water for irrigation when it is most needed. Population pressure will mean that less suitable land will be increasingly brought into production. The likelihood of crop failures due to drought or frost will increase; leading to local famines unless supplies can be obtained through trade.

Long-run sustainability in food production is most threatened in developing countries. If trade is inhibited, developing countries will have to attempt to become more self-sufficient. This will reduce the likelihood that their agricultural resource base can be managed in a sustainable fashion, leading to a reduced production capacity in the future.

It seems clear that strong rules for international trade in agricultural products will be of considerable importance in the future. As a result, it is important to understand the WTO and how it operates. It is also important to understand the concerns of the major players in international agricultural trade and their negotiating positions. It is somewhat ironic that at the outset of the new millennium, the agricultural trade policies of many countries, both developed and developing, are dominated by protectionist concerns and an 18th century mercantilist perspective. Of course, developed countries have always viewed trade policy for agricultural commodities as an adjunct to their domestic agricultural policies. The prime goal of those policies has been to slow down the pace of the technologically induced exit from farming that has been going on for at least a century. This perspective dominates the agenda of both importers and exporters. Imports are seen as increasing the pace of exit and counter to the goals of agricultural policy. Exports are perceived as good because they slow down the exit process and help in the attainment of domestic policy goals. This often leads to apparently contradictory negotiating positions for countries that both import and export.

The WTO will have to deal with all these conflicting currents. It is one of the linchpins in the performance of the global agricultural system in meeting the increasing demand for food in the first part of the 21st century. The negotiations that began in the new century are important because they will set the stage for the next 25 years, and possibly beyond.

1.2 THE WORLD TRADE ORGANIZATION

It is a common mistake to perceive the WTO as a law-making and enforcement institution similar to a domestic legal system. It is not. It is an international organization that countries voluntarily agree to join. They can, if they so wish, withdraw from it. It has no coercive powers and all the countries that have chosen to become members have voluntarily accepted its rules. Hence, while it may be politically advantageous for politicians or advocates of trade policy positions to claim that 'the WTO has made their country' do this or that, it is simply not true. Domestic politicians have been extremely careful not to relinquish their ability to extend protection from foreign competition to their domestic constituents. This is a central element of national sovereignty, and closely guarded. The WTO is a political compromise. As a result, domestic politicians have also insisted that an 'out' be enshrined in the WTO – when domestic political pressure for protection becomes too 'hot' for them to bear, they can exercise the option of ignoring their WTO commitments.

The entire history of the GATT organization, and more recently the WTO which succeeded it, can be seen as a long process of raising the cost to domestic politicians of choosing to use the 'out' – of deciding to ignore their WTO commitments. The cost of ignoring WTO commitments is to accept retaliation. *Accepted retaliation* is one of the central principles of the WTO (Kerr and Perdikis, 1995). It means that if a country chooses to ignore its WTO commitments, then those other members of the WTO whose trade has been negatively impacted can seek compensation equal to the value of the trade loss or, if that cannot be agreed, impose retaliatory tariffs on products imported from the offending country. The offending country accepts that retaliation and waives the right to re-retaliate. This prevents the 'beggar thy neighbour' trade wars that destroyed the international trading system between the two world wars and deepened and lengthened the Great Depression of the 1930s.

A second central WTO principle is *non-discrimination*. It means that members of the WTO must treat all other members equally. The most common example of this principle is the extension of *most favoured nation* tariff rates to all members of the WTO. This means that a country that joins the WTO agrees to extend the lowest tariff rate it charges any (*most favoured*) country on a particular customs category of goods to all other members. Of course, being allowed access to all members' markets at the lowest rate provides a strong inducement for countries to join the WTO. However, the principle of *non-discrimination* is also important in raising the cost of ignoring WTO commitments. If a country wishes to ignore its WTO commitments, say by raising tariffs, then it must raise them to all members of the WTO, which means that all countries have the right to retaliate. The larger the number of countries that can retaliate, the greater the domestic costs of choosing to ignore WTO commitments. This prevents countries targeting individual or weaker trading partners when faced with breaking their WTO commitments.

The third major principle of the WTO is *transparency*. This means that there can be no secret deals. All trading arrangements negotiated between countries must be brought to the WTO where other members are allowed to scrutinize them. *Transparency* thus supports the principle of *non-discrimination*.

The reason for negotiating rules for trade is sometimes lost in the nationalistic rhetoric which surrounds trade disputes between countries. It is not countries that engage in international trade, it is firms. Firms identify commercial opportunities in other countries and engage in transactions with firms in another country. It is the bane of international commerce that, while a transaction involving a firm in Iowa selling beef to a firm in California seldom elicits a comment, when that same Iowa firm wishes to enter into a transaction to provide beef to a firm in London, all manner of parties feel they have a right to comment or to become involved. As suggested above, domestic politicians have guarded their ability to extend protection from foreign goods jealously. Domestic politicians would like to have extremely flexible rules for trade. However, flexible rules greatly increase the risk for those firms that wish to engage in international commerce. Poor protection from the capricious use of trade barriers by politicians puts investments made to take advantage of foreign markets at risk and inhibits the ability to take advantage of mutually beneficial commercial opportunities. Firms engaging in international commerce, therefore, desire strong rules for trade.

Arguments for protection on the basis of the national good have been largely discredited in economic theory (Perdikis and Kerr, 1998) and most politicians accept the proposition that trade liberalization is welfare enhancing. Hence, they are generally supportive of improving the security of international transactions – except when faced with strong local pressure for protection. The WTO embodies this difficult political compromise between the desire to support firms engaging in international commerce with strong rules for trade and the need, at times, to extend protection to domestic constituents.

The cost of ignoring WTO commitments has been raised over time. This has been accomplished in two ways. First, the number of countries which belong to the WTO has been expanding. Second, the number and types of international activities that are subject to WTO discipline has been extended. For example, one of the major reasons for the transformation of the GATT organization into the WTO at the Uruguay Round was to extend WTO principles to additional, and increasingly important, areas of international commerce – services and the protection of intellectual property. The GATT was constituted to provide rules of trade for goods and could not easily be extended to handle other areas of international commercial relations. As a result, it was decided at the Uruguay Round that two new agreements would be negotiated, the General Agreement on Trade in Services (GATS) and the Agreement on Trade Related Aspects of Intellectual Property (TRIPs). It was also agreed that a new international organization would be put in place to administer the three agreements – the GATS, the TRIPs and the original GATT. Although the GATT, as an organization, ceased to exist, the Agreement is still in force to govern the trade in goods. The GATT is now administered by the Goods Council of the WTO. The GATS is administered by the Services Council and the TRIPs by the Intellectual Property Council.

The WTO handles disputes arising from the three agreements. The WTO's dispute settlement system is much stronger than the previous GATT disputes mechanism and represents another example of raising the cost of ignoring international trade commitments. Under the GATT dispute system, all countries, including the country accused of ignoring its commitments, had to agree to have the dispute heard by a GATT Panel. In effect, other than the pressure which could be brought to bear through moral suasion, countries were able to avoid having their actions judged by the GATT.

Under the new WTO dispute resolution system, only one country need complain for a case to go a Panel. In addition, there are strict timetables specified to prevent tactical delays in establishing Panels, appealing Panel decisions or implementing Panel judgements, which again act to reduce the ability to strategically avoid the costs associated with ignoring WTO commitments.

Another area where it was possible to avoid the costs associated with ignoring international commitments prior to the Uruguay Round was trade in agricultural goods. In the early years of the GATT, at the insistence of the United States, a number of *waivers* were granted which exempted agricultural products from the set of rules for trade that had been negotiated. In particular, *waivers* had been granted on the use of export subsidies and non-tariff barriers to trade. This meant that a special set of rules could be applied in agriculture. Export subsidies are generally banned in the GATT. Prior to the Uruguay Round, agricultural export subsidies could be used as long as they did not result in the subsidizing country capturing 'more than an equitable share of the international market' (Kerr and Perdikis, 1995) in the subsidized commodity. As 'more than an equitable share' could not be operationally defined, this meant that export subsidies on agricultural commodities could be used virtually without constraint.

In the general WTO/GATT rules it is agreed that all trade barriers should be converted to tariffs. This is because tariffs are the least trade-distorting method of restricting imports. Tariffs are a fixed tax imposed on products entering into a country's customs territory. In the case of GATT tariff commitments, it means that the tariffs are *bound* at agreed levels. Agreeing to bind tariffs means that the country will not raise its tariff levels in future. Having tariffs fixed and applied in a non-discriminatory manner means that the lowest cost supplier(s) will be those that export to the country. If the relative competitiveness of firms changes over time, the ability to export will automatically move to the most efficient foreign supplier. Further, if a foreign firm increases its competitiveness relative to firms in the importing country, it will gain a larger portion of the market. Hence, tariffs are the least trade-distorting method of restricting trade. In contrast, import quotas – quantitative restrictions on the amount of a product allowed to be imported – must be apportioned among exporters. This is a bureaucratic process which does not ensure that the market will be supplied by the lowest-cost exporting firm. Variable levies (adjustable border taxes) and import quotas also protect the importing market from fluctuations in international markets and may increase the variability in prices faced by exporters. Prior to the Uruguay Round, to protect their markets from the instability that characterizes many agricultural markets, a *waiver* was granted to allow importers to use import quotas and variable levies.

By the mid-1980s, the extensive use of export subsidies, large expenditures on domestic support for farmers and the widespread adoption of non-tariff barriers had led to severely distorted international markets for major agricultural commodities and a virtual trade war between the United States and the European Union – a trade war that threatened to spill over into non-agricultural sectors. In an attempt to defuse the situation, it was agreed that the rules for agricultural trade would be re-integrated into the general GATT rules for trade during the Uruguay Round of negotiations. The negotiations on agriculture were particularly acrimonious, however, and were one of the reasons why the Round took seven years. A number of issues remained outstanding near the end of the Uruguay Round. To bring closure to the Round, it was agreed that negotiations on the outstanding issues would begin again no later than the end of 1999.

Essentially, what was agreed in the Uruguay Round Agreement on Agriculture (URAA) was that, while the principle of full integration of agriculture into the WTO was accepted, there would be a transition period. The length of the transition, however, was not specified. What was agreed in terms of limits on, for example, export subsidies and domestic levels of support for farmers, represents a step on the way to the full integration of agriculture into the WTO. The next step is the subject of the negotiations that began in 2000.

The WTO is an evolving organization. In part, this evolution stems from the process of implementing and operationalizing the new institutional structure put in place as a result of the Uruguay Round agreements. The WTO is also evolving as a result of the continuing process of negotiation. To date the process has generally been trade liberalizing with the long and slow removal of trade barriers and increases in the probability that costs will be incurred if existing commitments must be ignored. Progress has been difficult to achieve and nowhere more difficult than for trade in agricultural commodities. The Uruguay Round set the stage for the full integration of agriculture into the WTO. Many difficult questions remain, however, and this is the true legacy of the Uruguay Round.

1.3 THE URUGUAY ROUND AND ITS LEGACY

1.3.1 Integration of Agriculture into the WTO

While it was agreed to bring agriculture within the general WTO framework at the Uruguay Round, the negotiations did not lead to full integration of agricultural trade into the broader international trading system. Instead, agriculture was allowed a period of transition. The length of the transition was not specified and further negotiations will determine the pace of agriculture's convergence with general WTO disciplines. Full integration of the trade rules for agriculture into the WTO should be perceived as a goal accepted by the contracting parties to the WTO rather than as something to be accomplished within a set framework. In an attempt to ensure that progress towards that goal would continue to be made, the negotiators of the Uruguay Round mandated that agricultural negotiations were to continue no later than the end of 1999. Issues such as export subsidies, market access, domestic subsidization of agricultural producers and food security for developing countries remain major areas for further negotiations. The important agricultural trading powers have been developing their positions over the last few years and making changes to their trade regimes and domestic agricultural policies to support their negotiating positions. As yet there appears to be little common ground, suggesting that the renewed agricultural talks will be as difficult as the last. The pace at which agricultural trade will be integrated into the WTO remains a contentious issue and was a major stumbling block at the Seattle Ministerial Meeting of the WTO at the end of 1999. The United States and other major agricultural exporting countries were pushing for a timetable for full integration, but the European Union only wanted progress to a further stage to be on the agenda for negotiations.

It is also important to keep in mind that concessions on a specific issue can be traded off for concessions on other issues in the dynamics of international trade negotiations. Thus, a change that might appear detrimental when viewed in isolation may well be a small thing to trade off against a major concession elsewhere. This is particularly true given that there is now considerable economic theory to suggest that a country may be better off by unilaterally reducing its trade barriers under a range of industrial structures. Even if unilateral liberalization is likely to be welfare enhancing, concessions may still be a useful bargaining chip in negotiations.

There are three central issues that must be addressed in the negotiations mandated for 2000. These are the issues of export subsidies, market access and trade-distorting domestic subsidies.

1.3.2 Export Subsidies

Export subsidies are those where receipt of the subsidy is tied directly to the product being exported. There is a corresponding import measure, the tying of the receipt of subsidies to the use of domestic inputs in preference to imports of the same inputs. The latter is much less discussed in the trade literature. Both practices are considered unacceptable under general WTO/GATT rules. Almost all subsidies are likely to be trade distorting (Kerr, 1988). The long and unsuccessful search by agricultural economists to find *de-coupled* subsidies (those not associated with a supply response) ended in an arbitrary 'box' system that categorizes subsidies as to their political acceptability. Export subsidies were considered unacceptable regardless of their actual trade-distorting effects. In the WTO, they are prohibited, or in the *red box* category and a country found to have a subsidy in this category must immediately withdraw it. However, the URAA provided a transition exception for this category of subsidies on agricultural commodities.

In the long period prior to the Uruguay Round when agricultural trade was granted an exemption from many GATT disciplines, export subsidies on agricultural products were allowed and could be used virtually without limit due to the vague wording of the upper bound restrictions – 'not more than an equitable share of the international market' (Kerr and Perdikis, 1995). As a result, a number of countries, particularly the European Union, had built up large surplus disposal programmes based on export subsidies. The domestic agricultural policy reforms required to bring domestic supply and demand into balance were politically impossible in the European Union. The Uruguay Round compromise was to limit the use of export subsidies and somewhat reduce aggregate expenditures. New export subsidy programmes were prohibited. Members agreed that developed economies would be required to reduce expenditures on export subsidies by 36 per cent, with 1986–90 levels as the base period for the reductions. The volume of products exported under subsidy was to be reduced simultaneously by 21 per cent over the same period. These reductions were to take place over six years.

For developing countries, outlays on export subsidies were to be reduced by 21 per cent; export volumes subject to subsidies were to be reduced by 14 per cent over a ten-year period. Least developed countries were not required to make any adjustments.

It should be clear that these controls are only a tentative step on the road to integration into the WTO. Sixty-four per cent of the 1986-90 expenditures on export subsidies remain in some developed countries and almost 80 per cent in developing countries. There is still a long way to go until full integration.

While the United States will start the negotiations by insisting that export subsidies be eliminated, it is generally accepted that this will still not be possible in the European Union. The negotiations concern the amount by which export subsidy expenditures should be reduced and how closely countries will be tied to commodity-by-commodity commitments versus the flexibility provided by more general targets. General targets allow countries to average their subsidy commitments over a range of commodities. This means that politically sensitive commodities can continue to be subsidized at rates in excess of the average.

1.3.3   International Access to Markets

The general WTO/GATT rules mandate that all trade-restricting policies be converted into tariffs that give an equal degree of protection. Tariffs imply unlimited access to an importer's market for any foreign supplier that can be competitive at its supply price plus the tariff. The possibility of this degree of open access was not acceptable to many agricultural importers at the Uruguay Round. Further, tariffs (unlike the quantitative restrictions that they replace) do not provide protection from fluctuating international prices. Full exposure to the price variability exhibited by many international markets for agricultural commodities was not acceptable to a number of major agricultural importers. On the other hand, as international prices fluctuate, tariffs can completely shut out imports if prices are high. This could mean that products that had guaranteed access under the old import regime would have less access once the conversion to tariffs was made.

The compromise reached in the Uruguay Round was the institution of tariff rate quotas (TRQs) – sometimes called tariff quotas (TQs). These allow access up to a pre-specified quantity to a nation's market at low (or zero) tariff rates. Beyond the pre-specified (quota) quantity, higher and often prohibitive tariff levels apply on additional quantities of imports. The result is guaranteed access up to the quota quantity for efficient exporters. Minimum access levels at the low, within-quota rates were set at 3 per cent of domestic consumption, rising to 5 per cent in six years. Again, the convergence to general WTO disciplines was partial. Where tariffication (the conversion to tariffs) was made without the use of TRQs, it was agreed that tariffs would be reduced by 36 per cent from their declared levels.

While the agricultural exporting countries would like TRQs to be converted to simple tariffs at the new round of negotiations, this is unlikely to happen. Instead, negotiations will centre on increasing market access by expanding the quotas and/or lowering the over-quota tariff rates. These negotiations will be similar to the normal multilateral tariff-offer system that has characterized the long process of tariff reductions through the various GATT rounds.

Tariff rate quotas, like any system of quantitative restrictions, have to be administered. The limited import quantities have to be distributed among exporting firms and, possibly, trade partners. Exporting firms have complained that the process for distributing the quota portions of TRQs in many of the imposing countries is not transparent. Even if the market is allowed to determine the export supplier, this may lead to timing problems when the limited low-tariff quota quantities are used up early in the year, effectively shutting out exports for the remainder of the year. This can lead to commercial disruptions and raise the risk to food processors of using imported inputs (Gillis et al., 1985). Further, the distribution of TRQ quotas can impart considerable benefits to those firms that acquire the right to import. They have a vested interest in the system remaining in place and can be expected to lobby their governments hard for the retention of TRQs.

Another important market access issue relates to the value at which quantitative restrictions are converted to tariffs. As there is no standardized method for the conversion, countries have been able to impose prohibitive tariffs. A number of countries feel that this has denied them the market access they expected from the Uruguay Round. Further, the high post-conversion tariffs have allowed counties to practice 'dirty tariffication' whereby they impose tariffs at lower rates than their *bound* maximums. This allows them to alter the actual tariff rates on the basis of market conditions, effectively isolating domestic producers from international market fluctuations (and indirectly increasing the price variability experienced by exporters). Dirty tariffication gives the imposing countries what amounts to the use of *variable levies*, which were banned at the Uruguay Round. Exporting countries can be expected to push for lower tariff rates and a standard method of tariff conversion.

1.3.4 Domestic Levels of Support for Agriculture

At the Uruguay Round, WTO members agreed on a set of relatively arbitrary criteria regarding the acceptability of government subsidy policies. The absence of a tight economic definition of what constitutes a trade-distorting subsidy arises from two sources. The first is that all subsidies that apply to traded goods will distort trade in the long run. It is not possible to define truly 'de coupled' subsidies (those that do not affect supply). The second is that governments are not willing to give up the right to subsidize; it is one of the things that governments do. Domestic politicians would never accept a prohibition on their ability to subsidize in the name of international trade discipline.

The result has been a compromise. Subsidies would be grouped into three categories sometimes denoted as traffic-light-coloured boxes. Export subsidies, as discussed above, are prohibited (red box or GATT red) subsidies. There are also non-actionable (green box) subsidies, which governments are permitted to use and are not subject to retaliation – they are not countervailable. These tend to be broad-based (non-industry-specific) subsidies. Education and research subsidies are the most commonly referred to, but subsidies for regional development and environmental retrofitting, for example, are in the green box. No tight definition is given, but an illustrative list is provided – a list that can be added to or amended. The third grouping – amber/yellow box or actionable subsidies – are those which can be subject to countervail if certain conditions are met. The subsidy must cause injury to the complaining trading partner or subject it to 'serious prejudice'. The possibility of serious prejudice is automatically assumed if the *ad valorem* subsidization of a product exceeds 5 per cent. If a subsidy is not green or red box and exceeds 5 per cent of the value of the good then it is up to the subsidizing country to prove that its trading partner is not injured. This is a shift in the burden of proof to the subsidizing country. The 5 per cent *de minimis* provision is there to prevent nuisance countervail actions.

In the case of agriculture, some forms of direct subsidies, those that are not tied to future output, are considered to be 'green box'. For actionable subsidies, instead of moving to the *de minimis* levels of the general WTO rules, developed country governments agreed to reduce their total aggregate levels of support by 20 per cent over the six-year implementation period. Developing countries agreed to a 13.3 per cent reduction. However, a number of what would normally be actionable subsidies are excluded from the calculation of the *Total Aggregate Measure of Support*. These programs are sometimes denoted 'blue box' subsidies. While the presence of the blue box has made the reductions in domestic subsidies less painful for many countries, the composition of what should be in the blue box has become a contentious issue for the next round of talks on agriculture. Clearly, there is a long way to go before agriculture's subsidy regimes conform to general WTO disciplines.

Since the Uruguay Round, countries have been altering their domestic support policies for agriculture in ways that they think will make them compatible for inclusion in the green box of acceptable subsidies (Zampetti, 1995). Nevertheless, these subsidies will affect output at least in the long run: the greater the number of policies allowed into the green box, the more a country will export or the less it will import in the long run. Trade partners are likely to be dissatisfied in either case. As a result, there is likely to be considerable wrangling over the types of programmes that actually qualify for green box status.

Whatever the outcome of the green box arguments, the aggregate levels of agricultural support will be the subject of negotiations. As suggested above, the blue box compromises from the Uruguay Round will be important because they will determine what subsidy expenditures must be included to determine the aggregate level of support. There will also be difficult negotiations over commodity-specific commitments versus the flexibility imparted by multi-commodity averaging.

1.4 THE NEW ERA OF AGRICULTURAL TRADE DISPUTES

The world has moved on in the years since the end of the Uruguay Round and new trade issues have come to the fore. While the problems associated with integrating agriculture into the general WTO disciplines will remain an important part of new discussions and continue to vex negotiators, a host of new problems will vie with them for the centre stage. Some of the new problems in agriculture have arisen as a result of technological advances. Agricultural biotechnology was not considered a major problem at the Uruguay Round because it had not reached the stage of commercialization. The regulation of the fruits of biotechnology, genetically modified foods, has become a major domestic issue in a number of countries and differences in domestic approaches to regulation have led to potential new trade disputes – particularly between the United States and the European Union (Kerr, 1999).

The WTO recognizes only one source of pressure for protection – domestic producers. Resistance to imports of genetically modified foods, however, has arisen largely from consumers. Countries attempting to react to consumers' demands for protection have been forced to use the existing mechanisms, which are primarily aimed at preventing abuse of health and safety rules by politicians wishing to extend protection from imports to producers. These mechanisms are inappropriate for dealing with consumer demands for protection (Perdikis and Kerr, 1999). While genetically modified foods have the potential to lead to a major international confrontation, consumers have begun to question a broad spectrum of imports. Consumers have become interested in how the foreign goods sold in their markets are produced – animal welfare on farms, leg-hold traps, tuna harvesting methods, child labour, multinationals with practices some consumers consider questionable and so on. There has already been a major failure at the WTO over consumer-based protectionism, with the European Union choosing to accept retaliation rather than allow the import of North American beef produced using growth hormones (Roberts, 1998). In a similar fashion, environmentalists have been strident in asking for protection from goods produced in ways they perceive as unacceptable (Kerr, 2000). Accommodating these alternative demands for protection will be a major challenge at the next round of trade negotiations (Perdikis and Kerr, 1999).

The revolution in agro-biotechnology has the potential to lead to another major conflict at the WTO. A significant proportion of the value of goods produced using agro-biotechnology arises from the intellectual property embodied in the goods. At the Uruguay Round, the new WTO was given responsibility for the international protection of intellectual property through the TRIPS agreement. The WTO intellectual property system is untried and, given the incentives for piracy that agro-biotechnology would seem to present, disputes are bound to arise (Kerr,

Hobbs and Yampoin, 1999). The retaliation mechanisms built into the WTO to induce compliance with TRIPS appear to be ill-designed to accomplish their objective (Yampoin and Kerr, 1998). As a result, developed countries may wish to re-open the TRIPS for re-negotiation.

At the Uruguay Round, the focus on integrating those aspects of trade policy where agriculture had enjoyed waivers meant that some longstanding issues were shoved aside and not addressed. One of these was the treatment of contingent protection measures – anti-dumping and countervail – in the WTO. Anti-dumping concerns 'unfair' trading practices of private firms, while countervail pertains to the 'unfair' use of subsidies. The institutional mechanisms for administering anti-dumping and countervail actions are poorly grounded in economic theory and open to abuse. As WTO disciplines on the use of subsidies and inhibitors of market access begin to constrain governments' ability to provide relief to their agricultural sectors, they are likely to begin to rely increasingly on contingency protection actions. For agricultural commodities that are subject to cyclical markets, one of the commonly used definitions of dumping – selling below the cost of production – is particularly inappropriate. At the Seattle Ministerial Meeting of the WTO, a number of countries were demanding that contingent protection measures should be on the agenda for negotiation.

There are now a large number of relatively effective regional trade organizations operating under the broad umbrella of WTO rules. While the operations of such organizations are supposed to be consistent with their WTO obligations, the relationship between regional trade organizations and the WTO is somewhat vaguely defined. Some regional trade organizations, particularly in developing countries, have chosen to exclude large segments of their agricultural trade. This appears to contravene the WTO requirement that 'substantially all trade' be included in regional trade organizations. There may be further difficulties as former command economies attempt to align their agricultural trade and domestic policy regimes with those of the European Union.

Finally, China and Russia wish to accede to the WTO. China's accession appears near while Russia's is further off. Given that these countries still rely heavily on state trading enterprises and have large state-owned sectors, their integration into the WTO may be difficult. Based on their relative size, however, they have the potential to alter the very nature of the WTO (Ceko and Kerr, 2000). Thus, their accession negotiations must be handled carefully.

Clearly there are a number of new issues that will have to be dealt with at future WTO negotiations. Before dealing with the issues still outstanding from the Uruguay Round or these new issues, a theoretical framework which can be used to assess the ramifications of changes to trade policy is required. This is the subject of the next chapter.

2. Modelling trade for policy analysis

2.1 APPROACHES TO TRADE MODELLING

Formal analysis of any change to international trading regimes should ideally be done using a highly disaggregated, dynamic, general equilibrium approach. A high degree of *disaggregation* of commodities and sectors is essential because trade policy tends to differ vastly from market to market both within broad sectors of the economy such as agriculture and even within narrower subsectors such as livestock operations or fruit and vegetables.

A *dynamic* approach is important because shifts in resource use and other adjustments in the economy do not take place instantaneously, or costlessly. A shock to a national economy, such as a reduction of trade barriers in the context of multilateral trade liberalization or their removal as a result of joining a regional trade bloc, will lead to disequilibrium situations while economic actors are adjusting to the changes to the trading regime. It is important to be able to understand the paths of adjustment so that public policies may be put in place to minimize the disruptions arising from the process of adjustment. It is also important to prevent inappropriate policies being put in place based on a snapshot of the economy which, while it may exhibit an undesirable set of outcomes, actually represents a temporary rather than a permanent state of affairs.

A *general equilibrium* approach is warranted because changes in trading regimes, such as multilateral trade liberalization and forming or joining a regional trade bloc, will entail the shifting of resources out of one set of economic activities into other activities. Gains from trade are expected to arise whenever there is a shift of resources from comparatively inefficient industries to comparatively efficient ones. Such shifts typically increase imports of the products for which domestic production has declined and increase exports of products for which production has expanded. By specializing in the production of products in which the economy has a *comparative advantage* or is comparatively efficient and trading some of this additional production for goods that were formerly produced less efficiently, a net gain arises for the country engaging in international trade. Hence, changes in imports and exports are less important than the shifting of resources because the latter is the true cause of gains from trade while the former is simply the symptom. General equilibrium analysis explicitly allows these changes in resource use to be accounted for when examining the impact of changes to trading regimes.

While the dissaggregated, dynamic, general equilibrium approach to modelling the outcomes expected from changes to trading regimes seems to be an attractive ideal, the approach is not particularly tractable. General equilibrium analysis can undoubtedly provide valuable insights into the underlying relationships associated with changes in trade policy, but its very complexity condemns it to the realm of the abstract. On the theoretical side, most general equilibrium modelling of international trade involves two sectors or industries. Such models have contributed vital broad insights into trade. Consider three examples. First, these models show why the gains or benefits from trade arise from comparative advantage or a lower relative cost rather than absolute advantages based on factor productivity. Absolute advantages, while central to a country's standard of living, are by no means required for trade to be beneficial. Second, simple two-sector models show rigorously why trade policy changes tend to favour factors of production that are used intensively or exclusively in expanding sectors and harm those that are used in contracting sectors. Third, such models can be used to show how differentiated products, imperfect competition and economies of scale give impetus to the intra-industry trade – Australian wine for US wine – that is becoming increasingly prominent, especially within the manufacturing sector but also in processed foods. Each of these key insights forms part of the backdrop for the analysis in this book. Nevertheless, theoretical general equilibrium models themselves are of limited usefulness when considering major changes in trade regimes – such as multilateral trade liberalization – that involve complex changes to a wide array of trade and domestic policy instruments in many sectors.

Attempts to implement the general equilibrium approach empirically face two major practical problems. First, the resultant computational general equilibrium (CGE) models exhibit a high degree of aggregation and often incorporate *ad hoc* specifications for functional relationships. This means that their usefulness is limited to evaluating the interrelationships among a limited number of broadly defined sectors. While the aggregation process consolidates economically similar commodities, there are often major differences in the trade policies applied to such groups of commodities. This problem becomes acute when considering accession to a customs union, common market or economic union where there is a common external trade policy in addition to preferential trade. As the acceding country adopts the common external barriers, situations will often arise where some external barriers (and, thus, prices) rise while others fall within a single commodity aggregate. At the very best, the opposing quantity responses will be approximately netted out, leaving a rather vacuous average response for the aggregate commodity group.[1]

The second major problem with CGE models is that they tend to be 'black boxes' that lack transparency. Altering the input to the model, say by changing the trade policy regime, generates a new set of results (that is, a change in model output), but the logical linkages that explain why the particular result arises are often far from clear. Even less is known about dynamic paths of adjustment. Although CGE models do have a very useful role, they are far from being a panacea. It is also essential to engage in a detailed and disaggregated analysis of the impact of policy changes on individual disaggregated commodities.

The problems with implementing and interpreting general equilibrium models suggest that it is both necessary and desirable to consider an alternative, but complementary, approach. As with much of economic analysis, detailed examinations of specific industries are undertaken using comparative-static, partial equilibrium analysis. This means that the market for one product is examined in isolation. Since such individual markets are, after all, the building blocks of CGE models, this amounts to looking inside the black box by focusing on one market at a time.

When a market is viewed in isolation, information on inter-market resource shifting is lost as well as information on the inter-market effects of price and income changes. Paths of adjustment are also ignored as only pre- and post-change equilibria are compared. For many economic questions, the insights garnered from simple comparative-static, partial equilibrium analysis are acceptable compromises because the loss of information that arises from ignoring long-run dynamic adjustments and inter-market effects is not of sufficient importance to negate the usefulness of the analysis. To totally ignore the dynamic aspects of adjustment when considering changes to a trade regime like those that may be required of the agri-food sector in response to WTO negotiations may, however, lead to inaccurate projections and inappropriate negotiation positions. Nevertheless, it is common to ignore the differences between short-run and long-run effects of trade policy changes when doing comparative-static, partial equilibrium analysis because they tend to be qualitatively equivalent. The point that requires emphasis is that the quantitative differences can be dramatic. In the short run, firms tend to be constrained by both capital and landholdings, but in the long run these constraints are removed and, in addition, firms can enter or exit the industry.

In the remainder of the chapter, we first develop the simple short-run partial equilibrium model, and use it to evaluate trade policy. Then, we expand the model to include long-run issues and explore the long-run effects of policy.

2.2 A PARTIAL EQUILIBRIUM TRADE MODEL

The economic behaviour and equilibrium relationships that constitute the partial equilibrium trade model are overviewed in this section. There are three key behavioural components of the partial equilibrium trade model. These are the demand behaviour of domestic consumers, the supply behaviour of domestic producers, and the trading behaviour of foreigners who are located in the rest of the world.

We begin by examining the optimal behaviour of domestic consumers. Panel (a) of Figure 2.1 shows the demand curve, D, for a commodity such as pork. As the price of pork, P, rises, consumers are willing to purchase less and less. Consequently, the quantity demanded, Qd, declines and the demand curve for pork is negatively sloped. There is another way to view the demand curve. The height of the demand curve indicates what consumers are willing to pay for each successive tonne of pork. We call this the marginal willingness to pay, or marginal benefit. Suppose that the price is $P0$. If less than $Qd0$ tonnes are purchased, the marginal or extra benefit from purchasing another tonne of pork is higher than the price so that it makes sense to purchase more pork. Contrariwise, if more than $Qd0$ tonnes are purchased, the marginal or extra benefit from purchasing the last tonne of pork is lower than the price so pork consumption will fall. Consequently, the optimal purchases of pork are equal to $Qd0$ tonnes when the price is $P0$ dollars per tonne.

We measure the total benefit of $Qd0$ tonnes of pork by adding up the marginal benefits of each successive tonne purchased up to $Qd0$. This total benefit, or total willingness to pay, for $Qd0$ tonnes of pork is given by the monetary value of the sum of areas $a + b + c + e + f$ in panel (a) of Figure 2.1. Actual consumer expenditure, however, differs from this total willingness to pay. Since the price is $P0$ dollars per tonne and domestic consumers choose to buy $Qd0$ tonnes, they will spend a total of $P0 \times Qd0$ dollars. Thus, the actual expenditure on pork is equal to the sum of areas $e + f$ dollars in the diagram. Consequently, there is a net benefit or consumer surplus of areas $a + b + c$ dollars when $Qd0$ tonnes of pork are purchased at $P0$ dollars per tonne. The presence of this consumer surplus makes sense since consumers were not coerced into purchasing pork. The reason that people voluntarily purchase $Qd0$ tonnes of pork at a price of $P0$ is that it is beneficial for them to do so.

Now suppose that the price of pork rises from $P0$ to $P1$ dollars per tonne of pork. This gives rise to a reduction in the quantity from $Qd0$ to $Qd1$ tonnes. Total willingness to pay for $Qd0$ units falls from the sum of areas $a + b + c + e + f$ dollars to $a + b + e$ dollars in panel (a) of Figure 2.1. Actual expenditure changes from $e + f$ dollars to $e + b$ dollars.[2] Whereas the initial consumer surplus was the triangle-like area above the $P0$ price line and inside the demand curve comprizing $a + b + c$ dollars, the final consumer surplus is the smaller triangle above the $P1$ price line consisting of a dollars. Thus there is a loss, or negative change, in consumer surplus consisting of $b + c$ dollars. This not only reflects the obvious fact that consumers are made worse off by a price increase, but it also allows the damage that they suffer to be quantified – a monetary value equal to area b. We emphasize that the change in consumer surplus or consumer welfare can typically be represented by the area lost or gained between the two price lines and inside the demand curve.[3]

Now consider the supply behaviour of domestic pork producers shown in panel (b) of Figure 2.1. As the price of pork rises, production becomes more profitable and the outputs supplied by firms increase. Thus, the quantity supplied, Qs, increases, leading to a positively sloped supply curve, S, for pork. We assume that the industry is competitive in the sense that there are many pork producers, each with a small market share and an imperceptible effect on the market price. In such a competitive industry the price is equal to the extra or marginal revenue that a producer obtains from selling an additional tonne of pork. There is, of course, a cost of obtaining resources or inputs to production that are necessary to supply pork. We call the cost of bidding production inputs away from alternative uses the opportunity cost of producing pork. The height of the supply curve measures the extra opportunity cost or marginal cost of supplying each successive tonne of pork. As more pork is produced, the marginal cost typically rises, reflecting the fact that it becomes more difficult to obtain the underlying inputs from competing economic uses. Again, we see that the

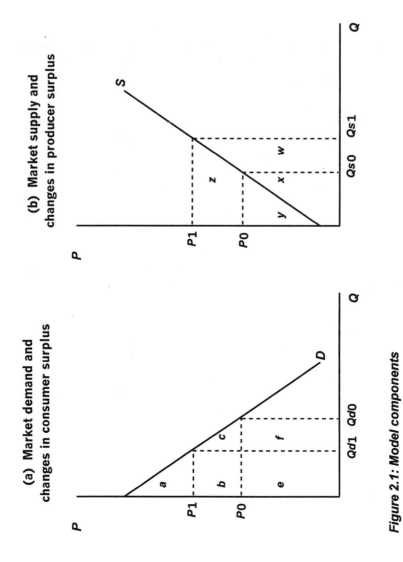

(a) Market demand and changes in consumer surplus

(b) Market supply and changes in producer surplus

Figure 2.1: Model components

supply curve is positively sloped. Further, in the short run there are constraints that preclude adjusting fixed factors such as capital or land use.

Indirectly, the presence of fixed factors prevents the entry or exit of firms in the short run. Thus, the relaxation of fixed factor constraints – both directly and indirectly by allowing new firms to enter or exit the industry – makes increases in output less costly in the long run than in the short run. The differences between the short and long run will be examined further in Section 2.5.

Suppose that the price of pork is $P0$ dollars per tonne in panel (b) of Figure 2.1. On the one hand, if the quantity supplied were less than $Qs0$, the marginal or additional opportunity cost of the last unit produced would be less than the marginal or extra revenue obtained, and producers would expand production. On the other hand, if the quantity supplied were more than $Qs0$, the marginal cost of producing the last unit would have exceeded the marginal revenue and producers would reduce output. Consequently, the optimal supply of output is $Qs0$ at the price of $P0$. The total opportunity cost of output $Qs0$ is obtained by adding up the marginal opportunity cost for each successive unit of output up to $Qs0$. This gives a total opportunity cost of the area beneath the supply curve or x dollars. On the other hand, the total revenue obtained by producing $Qs0$ is $P0 \times Qs0$ or $x + y$ dollars. Thus the total revenue exceeds the total opportunity cost and there is a net benefit to firms or a producer surplus of y dollars. Since pork producers voluntarily sell their product, the presence of such a producer surplus is hardly surprising. While the producer surplus definitely includes any producer profits, we will see in Section 2.6 that it also includes historic or inescapable costs and takes into account variations in the underlying returns to inputs or factors of production.

If the price now rises from $P0$ to $P1$ dollars per tonne in panel (b) of Figure 2.1, the industry output rises from $Qs0$ to $Qs1$ tonnes of pork. The total opportunity cost rises from area x dollars to $x + w$ dollars, while the total revenue rises from $x + y$ to $w + x + y + z$ dollars. Although the opportunity cost of obtaining the necessary resources to increase pork output from $Qs0$ to $Qs1$ is area w dollars, the additional revenue from the price increase is $z + w$ dollars. Thus, there is a gain of z dollars in producer surplus stemming from the price increase. Not surprisingly, an increase in price is beneficial to producers.

When domestic consumers and producers both have access to international markets, then we refer to the price in international markets as the world price. To clarify the essential issues, assume that there are no transport or transaction costs and, for the moment, ignore the wide array of policy measures that create differences between domestic and world prices. At high world prices, there will be an excess of supply over demand for pork that will lead to pork being exported. Thus, when the world price is $Pw1$ in panel (a) of Figure 2.2, $X1$ or $Qs1 - Qd1$ tonnes of pork will be exported. Conversely, at low world prices there will be an excess of demand over supply that will necessitate importation. In panel (b), $M0$ or $Qd0 - Qs0$ tonnes of pork is imported when the price is $P0$. If the world price happened to be equal to PA, the quantities demanded and supplied by domestic residents would balance and trade would be unnecessary.

The more pork foreigners import, the lower the world price they will be willing to pay. In other words, as the domestic economy exports more, the world price will fall. Conversely, as the domestic economy imports more, the world price will rise. The determination of the world price is considered in detail in Section 2.4. Generally, the rest of the world is much larger than any one domestic economy. Consequently, changes in the domestic market tend to cause only minor variations in the world price. Indeed, for small countries, these world price changes would be negligible. For most of the issues that need to be examined in relation to negotiations on agricultural trade, we need only mention the world price changes rather than explicitly incorporate them into the diagrammatic exposition. An important exception, where world price changes must be modelled explicitly, arises when analysing the implications of the negotiations relating to the control of export subsidies (Section 3.4).

The position of the domestic demand curve for pork is affected by the preferences and incomes of consumers and by the prices of related products. For most goods, an increase in incomes generates additional consumption and thus shifts the demand curve to the right. For such *normal goods*, an increase in consumer incomes, due say to an economic upturn, generates higher consumption at any given world price. This will reduce exports, cause a switch from exports to imports, or generate an increase in imports. In an economic downturn when incomes tend to fall, these effects would be reversed. However, some staples such as potatoes are *inferior goods* where consumption declines in response to an increase in income. For such goods an increase in incomes would reduce consumption at the going world price and thereby increase exports or reduce imports (or cause a switch from imports to exports).

If the world price of a substitute product such as beef were to rise, the demand curve for pork would shift to the right. Pork consumption would rise at the prevailing world price for pork and the domestic economy would

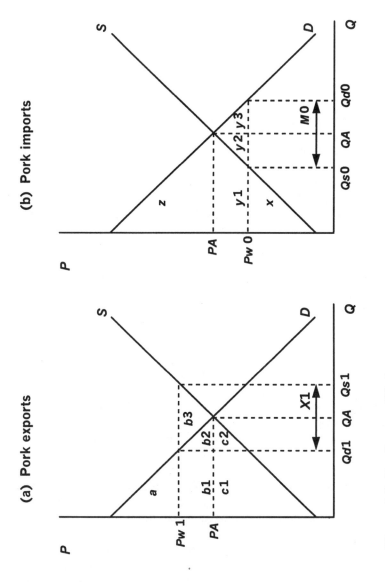

(a) Pork exports

(b) Pork imports

Figure 2.2: Trading equilibria

29

export less or import more. However, if the world price of a complementary good that is consumed together with pork were to rise, the demand curve for pork would shift to the left, consumption would decline, and exports would rise or imports would fall.

The position of the supply curve is affected by the underlying input or factor prices. Consider an autonomous increase in the price of an input, such as domestic labour, which is not caused by a variation in the market output of pork. Costs will rise, shifting the market supply curve to the left, lowering the output of pork at the prevailing world price and making producers worse off. Further, exports will fall and imports will rise (or the country will switch from importing to exporting). Since labour is not very mobile internationally, the impact on the world price is likely to be negligible. If we consider an increase in the price of an input that is internationally tradable such as feed, however, the world price of pork would tend to be pushed up as well. This would partially offset the impact on domestic producers.

Technological improvements have been a hallmark of agriculture over the last century. The green revolution of the 1970s and 1980s and current developments in biotechnology are but recent examples. Technological changes typically affect both domestic supply and the world price. Since a technological advance in pork production – such as the introduction of a new antibiotic – would reduce costs, output would increase and exports would rise or imports would fall at the initial world price. Further, those producers who were able to adopt the successful new technology would be very profitable, while producers who were committed to the old technology would be hurt and might ultimately go bankrupt. Since the new technology would be available throughout the world, however, the world price would be likely to fall. This would at least partially reduce the increase in output and the overall producer benefits. In the case of growth hormones, for example, consumers may not be indifferent, which would cause further complications associated with a demand reduction. Similar adverse consumer responses to biotechnology are considered fully in Sections 4.4 and 4.5.

The model can now be utilized to analyse changes in trade policy. In the next section we consider changes in trade policy caused by the implementation of tariffs and export subsidies. Following that, in Section 2.4, we consider more drastic policy changes where a market that was initially closed to trade is opened up to unrestricted trade.

2.3 USING A MODEL FOR POLICY – TARIFFS AND EXPORT SUBSIDIES

In this section, we put the partial equilibrium trade model through its paces to examine two important types of policy intervention in international agricultural markets. First, we will analyse the impact of a tariff imposed by an importing country. Thereafter, we will consider an alternative situation where an exporting country implements an export subsidy.

Suppose that Poland imposes a tariff (tax) on its imports of wheat. For simplicity we assume a simple flat rate or per unit tariff of T zloty per tonne. While the tariffs are also often assessed on an *ad valorem* or percentage basis, the substantive economic effects are the same. These effects are summarized in Figure 2.3. The world price, Pw, is the price at which imports of wheat can be secured on the international market. To clarify the essential relationships, we continue to assume that there are no transport or transactions costs. Prior to the implementation of the tariff, therefore, the domestic price or landed price is equal to the world price. At Pw, domestic consumers are willing to purchase $Qd0$ while domestic firms are only willing to supply $Qs0$. The difference, $Qd0 - Qs0$ is met by wheat imports.

After the tariff is imposed, the domestic price of imports rises to Ph or $Pw + T$. This becomes the price at which firms must compete with imports. The higher domestic price affords profit-maximizing firms the opportunity to expand output. In the market, domestic output expands from $Qs0$ to $Qs1$ as resources are drawn away from other sectors of the economy. However, the higher domestic price leads to a decline in consumption from $Qd0$ to $Qd1$. Consequently, imports fall to $Qd1 - Qs1$.

As the loss suffered by consumers due to higher prices is greater than the combined gain reaped by producers and the government, the change in trade regime is also assessed to be welfare reducing for Poland's domestic economy. The higher domestic price causes a gain in producer surplus and a loss in consumer surplus. In particular, the change in the value of consumer surplus is equal to a loss of $a1 + a2 + a3 + a4 + a5$ ($a1 + ... + a5$) zloty, while the change in producer surplus is a gain of area $a1$. The loss in consumer surplus exceeds the gain in producer surplus by $a2 + ... + a5$ zloty. The change in government revenue arising from the tariff is a gain of $a3 + a4$ zloty, which amounts to the height of the tariff multiplied by the quantity imported. Thus, there is an efficiency loss or a decline in real income from

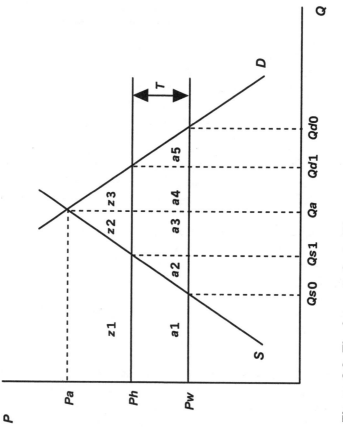

Figure 2.3: The impact of a tariff

the tariff. This is represented as a change in total surplus that is a *deadweight* or *distortionary loss* of $a2 + a5$ zloty.

Increases in the height of the tariff always serve to increase production but reduce consumption and imports at the given world price. Consequently, there are inevitably further gains in producer surplus (i.e., area $a1$ becomes larger), further losses in consumer surplus (that is, the sum of areas $a1 + \ldots + a5$ gets larger) and further distortionary losses (that is, areas $a2$ and $a5$ each increase). Tariff revenue given by areas $a3 + a4$ is subject to conflicting pressures, however, since more revenue per unit is collected on a smaller volume of imports. Thus as the tariff is slowly increased from zero to a height that prohibits trade, tariff revenue will initially rise but eventually declines.

When a smaller country implements a tariff, the change in world price is typically negligible. Consequently, no further analysis is needed. Suppose, however, that Japan implemented a tariff on rice.[4] Since Japan is a large trading country, the fact that Japanese rice imports are reduced leads to a lower world price for rice (that is, the reduced Japanese imports must be absorbed in other markets). Thus there is a favourable terms of trade effect for Japan that arises at the expense of the rest of the world as a whole in addition to the distortionary loss. If the tariff were kept sufficiently small, the terms of trade gain would outweigh the distortionary loss, resulting in an overall gain for Japan. Since the rest of the world suffers from an exactly corresponding terms of trade loss, there remains an overall efficiency loss affecting the world as a whole. In the next section, we argue that even large countries rarely conduct trade policy to try to obtain such national welfare gains. In fact, Japan's tariff on rice is set so high that it most definitely results in an overall reduction in welfare even though it is beneficial to Japanese producers.

We now turn to the case of a policy intervention in a market where the commodity is exported. Suppose, for instance, that Poland imposes an export subsidy on beef. An export subsidy – like a tariff – will raise the domestic price above the world price because domestic consumption in the exporting country is not subsidized. It is noteworthy that a tariff must be implemented in conjunction with the export subsidy to prevent cheap beef from the world market entering (or re-entering) the high-price domestic market. Thus a tariff equal to *ES* zloty per tonne would raise the domestic price from *Pw* to *Ph* in Figure 2.4. The subsidy becomes effective when product surplus to the domestic market arises at *Ph*. Since producers must

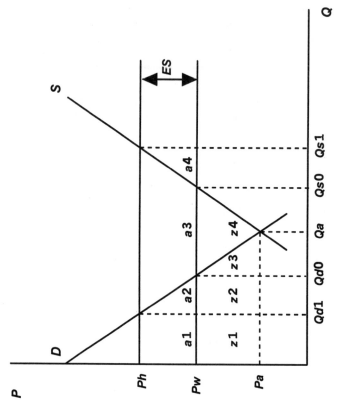

Figure 2.4: An export subsidy

earn *Ph* on this excess product, the government must spend *ES* per unit exported to make the product competitive at *Pw*.

The export subsidy is similar to the tariff in terms of the impact on domestic producers and consumers. The increase in the price from *Pw* to *Ph* increases output from *Qs*0 to *Qs*1 as resources, once again, are drawn away from other sectors of the economy. As a result of the higher domestic price, consumption drops from *Qd*0 to *Qd*1. Since the country is initially an exporter, these changes serve to increase exports rather than reduce imports. The export subsidy raises exports from *Qs*0 – *Qd*0, to *Qs*1 – *Qd*1. As in the case where a small country imposes a tariff, the overall impact on domestic welfare is negative. Producers gain *a*1 + *a*2 + *a*3 zloty in producer surplus, but consumers lose *a*1 + *a*2 in consumer surplus and the treasury loses (*Qs*1 – *Qd*1) × *ES* or *a*2 + *a*3 + *a*4 zloty in subsidy outlays. Thus, there is an efficiency loss of *a*2 + *a*4 zloty.

Increases in the height of an export subsidy cause further increases in output and exports, and further reductions in consumption at the given world price. Consequently, there are, inevitably, further gains in producer surplus (that is, area *a*1 + ... + *a*3 becomes larger), further losses in consumer surplus (that is, the sum of areas *a*1 and *a*2 gets larger), and further distortionary losses (that is, areas *a*2 and *a*4 each increase). Unlike raising tariffs, where the impact on government revenue is ambiguous, total outlays on export subsidies are certain to rise as export subsidies are increased. This is because of the combination of higher subsidies per unit and larger export volumes (that is, area *a*3 increases).

As in the case of the tariff, there is a negligible impact on the world price if a small country such as Poland implements an export subsidy. In the case of a large trading entity such as the European Union, however, the reduction in the world price arising from additional subsidy-induced exports can be significant. In the case of an exporting country, this would represent a terms of trade deterioration that would add to the negative impact on overall welfare. Clearly, the observed widespread use of export subsidies on agricultural commodities cannot be explained on the basis of attempts to improve national welfare. The underlying rationale for such export subsidies is investigated further in the next section. The impact of the export subsidies and retaliatory export subsidies of large trading entities such as the European Union and the United States on world prices is considered in depth in Section 3.4.

Tariffs and export subsidies share the common feature of increasing domestic prices and generating producer benefits at the expense of consumers. Price floors or support prices that apply to both producers and consumers afford similar protection to the domestic industry. We have seen that a tariff or like measure is an integral element of an export subsidy policy since it is necessary to deny consumers access to cheaper products on the world market. Similarly, a tariff will be required with a price support system. If the country remains on an import basis, as in Figure 2.3, a tariff is the only auxiliary policy that is necessary. However, if the country comes to be on an export basis, as in Figure 2.4, further auxiliary measures are necessary to deal with the surplus product that arises at the floor price. The government must intervene to buy up the surplus; thereafter, its options include storage, subsidizing exports and/or providing domestic or overseas food aid.

Figure 2.4 shows a situation where Poland is an exporter of wheat prior to the implementation of an export subsidy programme. It is certainly possible for a country to be on an import basis initially and to switch to exporting as a result of the tariff and export subsidy combination. This possibility is discussed further in Section 2.7. Of course, if either of the two sample trade measures were to be removed so that prices declined, outputs would be adjusted downward and resources freed up to return to other uses.

Levels of trade-related support to agriculture vary considerably across countries and commodities, as shown in Table 2.1. Here trade-related support measures include an array of policies, such as tariffs, export subsidies and floor prices. Broadly speaking, Japan tends to be more protectionist than the European Union and the European Union more protectionist than the United States. Generally, negative levels of trade-related support are indicative of policies that directly or indirectly tax exports.

2.4 GAINS FROM TRADE, WINNERS AND LOSERS, ADJUSTMENT COSTS AND VESTED INTERESTS

Some trade is, under almost any circumstances, better than no trade (autarky) for an economy as a whole. Even on a piecemeal or market-by-market basis, opening up trade is typically beneficial. This is true whether a country ends up importing or exporting the product in question. Consider a simplified world pork market where there are two countries, Europe and America. While there are, in reality, many importing and exporting countries that are aggregated to comprise the world market, Figure 2.5 shows the essentials of how the world price is determined. In the absence of trade, the equilibrium in Europe would be at a quantity of Qa tonnes of pork and a price of *Pa* dollars per tonne where European demand and supply are in balance. Similarly, in America the autarky quantity is Qa^* tonnes of pork and the autarky price is Pa^* dollars per tonne.

Table 2.1 Trade-related market price support in 1998 (%)

	European Union	United States	Japan
Wheat	11	−20	57
Maize	2	−14	0
Other grains	8	−15	31
Rice	35	−15	473
Oilseeds	0	−4	0
Sugar (refined)	210	76	78
Milk	125	115	245
Beef and veal	105	−10	42
Pig meat	12	−23	140
Poultry	22	−9	12
Sheep meat	35	0	0
Wool		13	0
Eggs	9	−9	18
Other commodities	47	2	139
All commodities	48	3	113

Formula: Consumer NAC −1.
Source: OECD, (1999).

In practice, producers and consumers in both countries may have access to international markets. The supply curves are drawn such that America is a lower cost producer of pork than Europe and therefore has a lower autarky price. As a result, Europe will tend to import pork and America will tend to export pork. We refer to the price in international markets as the world price. To clarify the essential issues, we assume that there are neither transport nor transactions costs, and we will initially ignore the wide array of policy measures that cause differences between domestic and world prices.

At world prices below *Pa*, there is excess demand for pork in Europe, representing desired imports. This excess demand or desired imports is graphed in the centre panel of Figure 2.5 as a demand for imports curve, *Dm*. Notice that the distance between the demand and the supply curve in the left panel of the figure is exactly equal to the distance from the vertical axis to the import demand curve in the centre panel. Thus, at lower prices more is imported. While there would be excess supply of pork and Europe would choose to export at prices higher than Pa, we will see that Europe will import in the trading equilibrium. If the world price is above Pa^*, there will be excess supply of pork in America, which represents desired exports. These desired exports of America give rise to the export supply curve, Sx^*, in the centre panel of Figure 2.5.

In Figure 2.5, there is a trading equilibrium at the world price of $Pw1$ dollars per tonne of pork where Europe's desired imports of $M1$ tonnes exactly balance with America's desired exports of $X1^*$ tonnes. At this world price, Europe consumes $Qd1$ tonnes of pork and produces $Qs1$ tonnes with the difference being the $M1$ tonnes that are imported. Meanwhile, America produces $Qs1^*$ tonnes, consumes $Qd1^*$ tonnes and, as we have seen, exports the difference of $X1^*$ tonnes.

Let us consider how the opening of trade affects overall welfare in America and Europe. The move to free trade leads to overall gains for the exporting country, America, but it also creates clear winners and losers. In the absence of trade in pork, the consumer surplus is equal to $f + g + h$ dollars and the producer surplus is equal to $j + k$ dollars. Opening trade at the world price of $Pw1$ leads to a decline in consumer surplus of $g + h$ dollars and an increase in producer surplus of $g + h + i$ dollars. Allowing exports of pork therefore generates a gain in total surplus of area i dollars. Since America becomes an exporter, the impact on producers is decisive in overall effect; the gain in producer surplus is unambiguously larger than the loss in consumer surplus.[5]

When only one market is being opened, there may be beneficial or harmful indirect effects on other markets from the price change on the liberalized market. For example, higher pork prices will generate indirect benefits (that is, more consumer surplus) from the consumption of substitute products such as beef and poultry, and indirect costs (that is, less consumer surplus) from the consumption of any complementary products. In the rare instance where the harmful indirect effects not only dominate the beneficial indirect effects, but also outweigh the direct gains that we have just examined, America could lose from liberalizing trade on a single market. If the entire economy were to move from autarky to free trade, there is a very strong presumption of overall gains from trade.[6] In such a situation, there would be direct benefits on each market that would in aggregate more than offset any adverse indirect benefits.

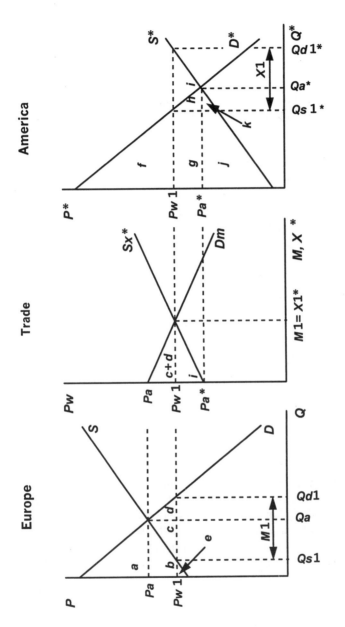

Europe

Trade

America

Figure 2.5: Mutual gains from trade

While it seems broadly sensible that there are direct gains from trade generated on an export market, perhaps it is more surprising to find that there are also net gains for the country that imports. In the European market that is being opened to imports, the consumers are the winners and the producers are the losers. Prior to trade, the consumer surplus is equal to a dollars and the producer surplus is equal to $b + e$ dollars. When trade commences, producers are hurt by the price reduction and experience a loss of producer surplus equal to area b dollars. Meanwhile, lower pork prices yield a benefit to consumers or a gain in consumer surplus given by $b + c + d$ dollars. Thus there is an unambiguous gain in total surplus to Europe from introducing free trade equal to $c + d$ dollars. Since Europe imports, the impact on consumers dominates; the consumers gain more than producers lose.[7]

Overtrading cannot be as beneficial as free trade when markets are competitive. As we saw in Section 2.3, the imposition of an export subsidy starting from a position of free trade resulted in a loss in total surplus of area $a2 + a4$ in Figure 2.4. The losses of the consumers (that is, area $a1$) and the government (that is, area $a2 + a3 + a4$) exceed the gain to the producers (that is, area $a1 + a2 + a3$). Even if the country is small, so that its export subsidy has no adverse effect on world prices, it loses from overtrading relative to free trade.

If the country is small and has no effective market power over world price, it will also lose from restricting trade starting from free trade. In Section 2.3 (Figure 2.3), we saw that Poland would lose areas $a2 + a5$ relative to free trade if it imposed a tariff on the beef market. The loss to consumers (that is, areas $a1 + ... + a5$) exceeded the gains to producers (that is, area $a1$) and the government (that is, areas $a3 + a4$). Since neither overtrading nor undertrading pays, free trade is a national-welfare-maximizing policy for a small country. In the current case of a large player, such as Europe, limited trade restrictions can be better than free trade, because of the induced decline in the world price that would arise from moving down and to the left along America's export supply curve, Sx^*, in Figure 2.5.

In agriculture, as in other sectors of the economy, national interests rarely drive trade-related policy exclusively, or even predominantly. Rather, policy tends to be driven by the interests of producers, input suppliers and owners (factor groups). They represent 'vested interests'. While governments tend to be relatively immune to proactive 'rent seeking' by factor and industry lobby groups, disadvantaged factor and producer groups that are already under stress and reacting to forces such as technological change tend to receive a more sympathetic hearing from governments. In practice, such pressures have been felt most acutely in sectors such as agriculture where there has been a long-term secular decline in employment. Within developed countries, similar pressures have also affected industries such as textiles, footwear and steel.

In reality, the producers within any industry are typically heterogeneous. At any point in time there are many vintages of technology in use. This is particularly true in agriculture. Further, since technologies tend to be embodied in physical, human and biological capital, it is often extremely costly for existing producers to adopt new technologies. In the absence of government intervention, therefore, the least technologically efficient producers often face bankruptcy. When technological change is rapid and demand responses to increasing consumer incomes are low, as is often the case in agriculture, there may be large numbers of such inefficient producers.[8] Bankruptcy and exit from an industry in reality entails substantial adjustment costs. Labour must undergo re-training and search for alternative employment while individuals experience capital losses on other productive assets. Rural to urban shifts often involve particularly traumatic lifestyle changes that constitute a further adjustment cost. Factors of production do not move freely from one sector to another.

Faced with financial ruin, inefficient producers often react by lobbying governments for support. Even when increased foreign competition is more of a side effect than root cause of long-term sectoral decline, it is often a convenient scapegoat. For instance, when a technological advance such as better pesticides or more disease resistant seed leads to falling world grain prices, it is natural for producers to lobby for protectionist measures that raise the domestic price above the world price. Since we take domestic price support as the criterion for protectionism, we include export-enhancing measures such as export subsidies as well as import-restricting measures such as tariffs.

Care must be exercised in identifying all producers as winners from this type of reactive protectionism. Protectionism reduces or removes the incentives for the least technologically efficient producers to move to alternative activities. As a result, producers who would otherwise have been forced to exit the industry will be able to remain in business. Such producers maintain a tenuous foothold in the industry, but they can hardly be classified as winners in an absolute sense. The real winners, therefore, are the technologically efficient producers who obtain windfall benefits from protection as well as technological advance.

Of course, the big losers from protectionism are consumers. Since consumer interests are widely distributed, individual consumers – especially those who are threatened by a single tariff – tend to invest little in lobbying against tariffs. A tariff on, for example, ice cream, which most consumers purchase only intermittently and which in any case does not represent a significant portion of a consumer's food budget, is simply not worth the consumer's time and effort to lobby against. Producer interests, however, are much more focused and so producers invest much more in lobbying for protection when their economic position becomes tenuous. As a result, domestic and trade policy directed at the agricultural sector tends to be driven largely by producer interests, especially the interests of inefficient producers, at the expense of consumers.

2.5 LONG-RUN VERSUS SHORT-RUN POLICY ANALYSIS

In this section, we return to the analysis of tariffs and export subsidies begun in Section 2.3. Using only the short-run competitive model to analyse changes to trade regimes is too simplistic and can lead to misleading conclusions. At a minimum, it is necessary to take account of the dynamic forces that are put in motion by a change to the trade regime. While the qualitative impact of either policy is the same in both the short and the long run, the quantitative impact can differ dramatically. This quantitative difference arises because the supply response to a change in the domestic price is larger in the long run.

Recall that both tariffs and export subsidies serve to protect the domestic industry by raising the domestic price above the world price. While a tariff increases the domestic price directly, an export subsidy also raises the domestic price because domestic consumption is not subsidized. Further, since consumers must be prevented from accessing cheaper products on the world market, a tariff or similar trade barrier is an integral part of an export subsidy policy.

Figure 2.6 aids in the analysis of protectionist policies. The representative firm, shown in panel (a), is taken to be one of a large number of identical firms. In the short run, the number of firms cannot be changed and fixed factors or inputs such as physical, human and biological capital cannot be varied. The presence of fixed factors implies that the additional or marginal cost of producing an extra unit of output rises as total output expands. Profit maximization requires that the marginal revenue or extra revenue obtained from producing an additional unit of output be exactly

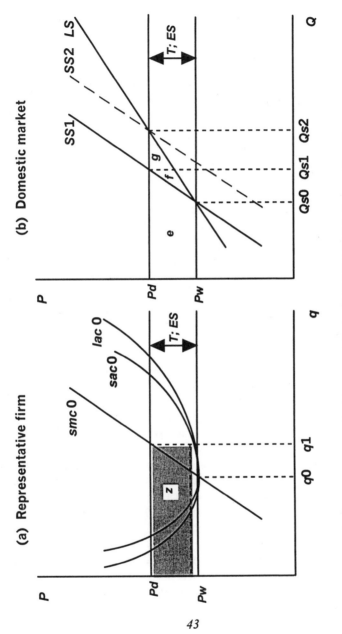

Figure 2.6: The long-run supply response to an increase in the domestic price

equal to the marginal cost. Since marginal revenue is equal to price for competitive price-taking firms, price is equal to marginal cost for profit maximization. This means that a firm's marginal cost curve is, in effect, its supply curve. Prior to the imposition of any policy measures, the domestic price is equal to the world price and the representative firm produces an output of $q0$. The industry's short-run supply curve, $SS1$, in panel (b) typically arises from summing the short-run marginal cost curves of all of the individual firms.[9] Consequently, the industry-wide domestic output is $Qs0$.

It is assumed that the market is initially in a state of long-run equilibrium at Pw where producers are only making normal profit. This means that producers will be making a return that is just sufficient to retain resources in the industry but not sufficient to attract additional resources into the industry. Consequently, the price is equal to the long-run, and for that matter the short-run, average cost (that is, $Pw = lac0 = sac0$) in panel (a). Notice that the economist's formulation of the opportunity cost of using capital – the so-called user cost – includes a normal rate of return on capital adjusted for the normal risks of production. This is in addition to the costs associated with depreciation whereby older machinery and buildings generally become less valuable as they gradually wear out. Suppose that the domestic price is raised above the world price through the implementation of a policy measure such as a tariff or export subsidy. The short-run adjustment to the trade shock means that firms move up their marginal cost curves to re-maximize their profits where marginal cost equals the new domestic price (that is, where Pd equals $smc0$). Output expands from $q0$ to $q1$, and the firm draws additional resources into production equal in value to the area under the marginal cost curve between these two quantities. Industry output increases from $Qs0$ to $Qs1$ in panel (b) and the total of additional resources drawn into the production of this good is equal to the area under the short-run supply curve, $SS1$, between $Qs0$ and $Qs1$. It should be noted that as this is partial equilibrium analysis it is not possible to discern where these additional resources are drawn from or the effects on individual resource markets. It is also not possible to discern the quantitative effect of the price increase on the markets of substitutes or complements of this product.

The increase in price means firms will make super-normal profits. Since Pd is greater than short-run average cost ($sac0$) at production level $q1$ in panel (a) of Figure 2.6, the representative firm will make a super-normal profit equal to the shaded area, or z dollars. The larger the short-run profits created, the stronger is the signal for entry and the faster will new resources be committed to increase production. Industry-wide super-normal producer profits are just one component of the industry's short-run producer surplus of *e* dollars shown in panel (b). In the short run, we have seen that producers face adjustment constraints whereby they cannot change at least some components of their capital (such as buildings). Since there is no alternative use for such fixed factors, there is no opportunity cost associated with their use. Thus, in addition to super-normal profits, the fixed costs or historic costs of such temporarily unadjustable factors enter into the producer surplus rather than the opportunity cost.[10]

This presence of super-normal profits will encourage new firms to enter the industry. Existing firms may also make investments to expand their outputs. The effect is to gradually shift out the short-run supply curve from *SS*1 to *SS*2, thereby returning the industry to its long-run supply curve, *LS*. As both entry and investment in new plant and equipment take time to put in place, the shift in supply will not be instantaneous. The positive slope of the long-run supply curve arises because the industry eventually faces increasing costs. As the industry as a whole expands, it bids up the price of inputs that it uses intensively, such as land. The industry also becomes a larger user of resources such as fertilizer, farm machinery and pesticides. In addition, the larger farm sector will require a larger processing industry with commensurate new investments.

There is a long-run gain in producer surplus equal to $e + f + g$ dollars in panel (b) of Figure 2.6. Since the firms do not earn any super-normal profits in the long run, this entire long-run increase in producer surplus is shifted back to inputs or factors of production such as land that are used intensively in the production of the commodity in question. Thus, the producer surplus accrues in the form of higher rents on inputs such as land. As we will see later in the book, the increase in the rental value of land shifts the firms' average and marginal cost curves upward such that the minimum long-run average cost is just equal to *Pd* in the final equilibrium where the industry produces *Qs*2. The higher rents on land reflect at least an imputed cost to producers since producers need not be landowners.

We can now explicitly incorporate the analysis of short-run and long-run supply behaviour into our analysis of trade policy. Figure 2.7 can be used to re-assess the impact of a Polish tariff of *T* zloty per tonne on wheat imports. As a result of the tariff-induced price increase there is a reduction in consumption from *Qd*0 to *Qd*1 tonnes and a loss in consumer surplus of $b1 + \ldots + b7$ zloty. In the short run, wheat output increases from *Qs*0 to *Qs*1 tonnes and imports fall from *Qd*0 − *Qs*0 tonnes to *Qd*1 − *Qs*1 tonnes. Since

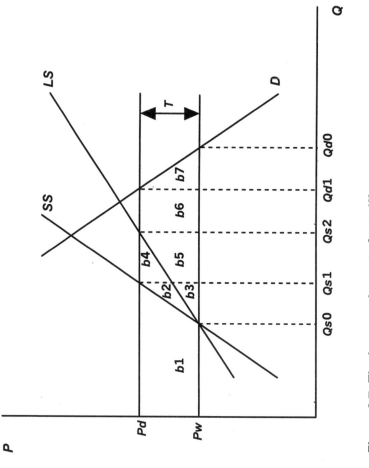

Figure 2.7: The long-run impact of a tariff

46

the short-run increase in producer surplus is $b1$ zloty and the short-run tariff revenue is $b4 + b5 + b6$ zloty, there is an efficiency loss equal to $b2 + b3 + b7$ zloty.

In the short run, wheat producers are earning (positive) super-normal profit. As we have seen, this acts as a signal for the entry of new producers. Over time, industry output gradually expands to the long-run level of $Qs2$ tonnes of wheat. Although consumption remains equal to $Qd1$, imports fall to $Qd1 - Qs2$. In the long run, the increase in producer surplus which accrues as rents is $b1 + b2 + b4$ zloty. The tariff revenue is $b6$ zloty. The loss in consumer surplus, however, is still $b1 + ... + b7$ zloty. The long-run efficiency loss from the tariff, $b3 + b5 + b7$ zloty, is larger than the short-run efficiency loss. The extra producer surplus of $b2 + b4$ zloty that arises in the long run is insufficient to compensate for the decline in government (tariff) revenue of $b4 + b5$ zloty. Thus, the short-run efficiency loss of $b2 + b3 + b7$ zloty is less than the long-run efficiency loss of $b3 + b5 + b7$ zloty.

Figure 2.8 shows the long-run impact of a Polish export subsidy on beef. The export subsidy is like the tariff in that the long-run impact on output exceeds the short-run impact because new firms enter the market. The export subsidy increases the domestic price from Pw to Pd. Output rises from $Qs0$ to $Qs1$ in the short run and onward to $Qs2$ in the long run. As a result, exports rise from $Qs0 - Qd0$ to $Qs1 - Qd1$ in the short run and onward to $Qs2 - Qd1$ in the long run. The short-run increase in producer surplus is $b1 + b2 + b3$ zloty and the long-run increase that accrues as an increase in rents is $b1 + ... + b5$ zloty. In both the short and the long run, consumer surplus falls by $b1 + b2$ zloty. The short-run budgetary outlay for export subsidies is $b2 + b3 + b4 + b6$ zloty, but this increases to $b2 + ... + b7$ zloty in the long run. Despite the fact that there is no further change in consumer surplus in the long run, there is a larger efficiency loss.

While the long-run increase in producer surplus exceeds the short-run increase by $b4 + b5$ zloty, the long-run outlay on export subsidies exceeds the short-run outlay by $b5 + b7$ zloty. Thus, the efficiency loss rises from $b2 + b4 + b6$ zloty in the short run to $b2 + b6 + b7$ zloty in the long run.

The immediate one-period benefit or loss to consumers is given by the change in consumer surplus, while the cumulative benefit or damage is obtained by taking the present value of the change in consumer surplus over the expected life of the policy. The immediate benefit or cost to producers is given by the short-run change in producer surplus. The long-term costs or benefits to the production side of the industry are somewhat more complex. When the supply price falls, the cumulative damage done to producers and

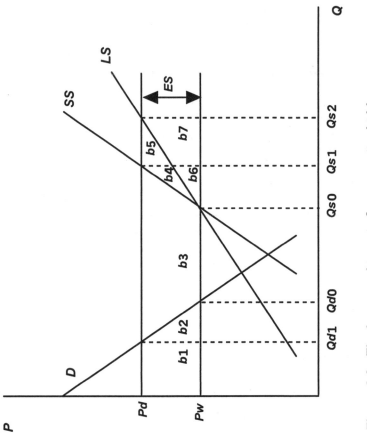

Figure 2.8: The long-run impact of an export subsidy

asset-holders exceeds the present value of the long-run losses in producer surplus because of the presence of temporary adjustment costs. Conversely, when the supply price rises, the present value of the short-run production-side benefits is less than the present value of the apparent long-run benefits, due again to the presence of temporary constraints on sectoral adjustment.

Even the addition of long-run considerations to the partial equilibrium analysis of changing trade regime leaves some important dynamic issues remaining. For example, the assumption that producers are in long-run equilibrium prior to the trade shock lacks realism when examining the agricultural sector. As we have seen, the agricultural sector is characterized by rapid rates of technological change and slow exit of non-competitive farmers. As a result, the sector can better be characterized as being in a constant state of disequilibrium. Rapid rates of technological innovation but with the adoption of technology spread over time means that individual firms will have different technological capabilities at any instant. As a result, they will have different productivity and different potential to make profit. At any given point in time, some proportion of farms is likely to be losing money while others are profitable. Agricultural policies, including trade policies, are put in place to raise the incomes of those farms that are not profitable. If policies, such as border measures that raise the price of farm output, do not support incomes solely on the basis of need, they will increase the profits of those farms that are already profitable.

2.6 CAPITALIZATION OF POLICY BENEFITS

Another vital insight that arises from approaching the examination of changes in a policy regime from a long-run perspective is that the benefits of policies will be capitalized into the value of relatively fixed assets. This can be illustrated in Figure 2.9, which depicts an efficient firm in an agricultural sector that will benefit from a policy change. Assume that the change in the trade or domestic policy regime leads to an increase in the price of the firm's output from Pw to Pd. For the moment assume that this is an industry (such as dairy farming in the European Union) where a quota is required before production can take place. Further, assume that the original farmer received the quota at no cost when the EU milk quota regime was initiated. We will show that this lack of an initial purchase price does not imply that the production quota has no value.

Suppose that the farm's long-run average cost curve was $lac0$ prior to the change in the trade policy regime and the implementation of production

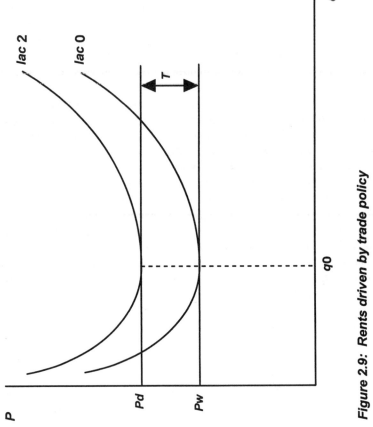

Figure 2.9: Rents driven by trade policy

50

quotas. This cost curve continues to represent production costs (and any other non-quota costs). The farm's production quota of $q0$ entitles it to revenue that exceeds production costs by the area given by $(Pd - Pw) \times q0$ in Figure 2.9. This difference between revenue and production cost is properly viewed as rent attributable to the production quota itself. Thus, the rent generated by a unit of quota is equal to $Pd - Pw$. Adding the cost of renting units of the quota for one period to the other costs of production in the period leads to the quota-inclusive long-run average and cost curve, *lac2*.

Let us examine the rents generated by production quotas from another perspective. As the quota is essential for production, it will be valuable to prospective buyers. Except in the rare cases where limited quantities of new quota are released to select groups such as 'young farmers', the only way a new entrant can produce is to acquire quota from an existing farmer who has quota. Assume that the existing farmer is willing to sell up and leave the industry. The question is how much new entrants will be willing to pay to acquire the quota above and beyond the purchase price of the farm? To begin with, consider how much an entrant would pay to rent the quota rights for one period. The question to ask, for example, is whether a prospective entrant would be willing to pay an amount that would increase its costs from *lac0* part of the way to *lac2* to rent the quota. At price Pd, the entrant would still earn super-normal profits and it would certainly be worthwhile to incur the additional costs of purchasing quota. Of course, another prospective buyer with the same technological efficiency would be willing to purchase the quota at a slightly higher cost. As long as there are sufficient numbers of buyers competing to acquire quota, the price of quota will rise until it reflects the costs associated with *lac2*. New entrants earn normal profits and so do not benefit from the programme.

This picture is too simple, however, because it shows the firm in only one production period. As the quota will be expected to generate rents in all future time periods, the purchase price of the quota will represent the discounted stream of future earnings. This is why EU milk quotas have high purchase values in some countries. The interest cost on the money borrowed to purchase the quota or the forgone interest on funds diverted into the acquisition of the quota represents an ongoing cost for the new entrant. In the most extreme case where the quota is expected to generate these rents in perpetuity, the purchase price or present value of $q0$ units of quota would be $[(Pd - Pw) \times q0]/r$, where r is the discount or interest rate.

Since the discount rate is a proper fraction, the purchase price of the milk quota is much larger than the one-period rents.[11]

Any attempt to lower the level of support – decreasing price below Pd – will lead to capital losses for new entrants who purchased quota rights, given that they have costs reflected in *lac*2. Clearly, entrants who joined the industry after the trade policy was imposed will resist any attempt to reduce programme benefits as it threatens the value of their assets. Firms that received their quotas at no cost will have had an increase in their asset value and will also resist any change. Banks may have lent against the value of the asset and face the risk of default as the borrower's debt obligations exceed the value of the asset used as security.

When quotas do not exist, the value of the programme that raises the domestic price from Pw to Pd will be capitalized into other fixed assets, usually land. The price of land is bid up as prospective entrants attempt to acquire land with which to enter into production. As we have seen, the inevitable bidding up of the price of fixed assets eventually chokes off the incentive to enter the industry and determines the limits of the long-run supply response. In Figure 2.7 we have seen that the additional rents to industry assets such as land that arise from the tariff are shown by area $b1 + b2 + b4$. In the long run, when entry eliminates super-normal profits, the entire change in producer surplus is shifted upstream and accrues as higher rents paid to inputs. It is these additional rents that get capitalized into higher land values. In the most extreme case where these rents are expected to continue in perpetuity, land values will increase by $[b1 + b2 + b4]/r$ because of the tariff. Analogously, in Figure 2.8, an export subsidy would increase rents by $b1 + ... + b5$ and increase asset values by up to $[b1 + ... + b5]/r$.

The lesson, again, is that any unwarranted expansion will be difficult to reverse after the fact, due to vested interests in the inflated value of the assets. Since trade policy benefits in many countries have in reality been capitalized into asset values, there is likely to be considerable policy inertia making the WTO negotiations on agriculture extremely difficult. This issue is addressed further in Chapter 3.

2.7   THE COMMON AGRICULTURAL POLICY OF THE EUROPEAN UNION: A LONG-RUN CASE STUDY

The models typically used by economists to examine the effects of policy and to forecast the impact of policy interventions are short-run models. In many cases this short-run (or timeless) approach is reasonable because the policy interventions do not lead to ongoing disequilibria and the 'comparative static' (which compares pre-change and short-run post-policy change positions) result is a new equilibrium. If one is not interested in the short-run paths of adjustment, comparing two static equilibria is often sufficient for policy analysis. Indeed, much of the training of economists who are expected to engage in policy analysis centres on deriving results using 'comparative statics'.

As suggested in the last few sections, if the trade policy intervention leads to an ongoing disequilibrium in a market, economic forces are set in motion which cannot be captured by short-run analysis using simple comparative statics. This may lead to unforeseen policy ramifications. In particular, if the policy intervention provides a stimulus for the entry of new production units and the capitalization of policy benefits, the long-run result may be quite different to that predicted by short-run analysis prior to the trade policy intervention. The evolution of the European Union's Common Agricultural Policy (CAP) can be interpreted in this manner. The designers of the CAP may simply have had the wrong model in mind. It is hard to believe that the European Union's agricultural policy was purposely designed to produce the current phenomenon of large annual surpluses, butter mountains and wine lakes, the need for export subsidies and other large-scale budgetary expenditures, land values that reflect capitalized policy benefits, and overinvestment in the agro-input and food-processing sectors. The evolution of the CAP points to the pitfalls of ignoring long-run economic forces when putting trade policy measures in place.

A stylized representation of the evolution of the CAP is depicted in Figure 2.10. Of course, a model is a simplification and a large number of short-run market fluctuations and longer-term policy refinements and sector variations are ignored. The European Union is a common market, which means that external trade barriers must be harmonized among the member countries. It also means that that there can be no artificial barriers to the movement of goods between member countries. In terms of the CAP, the latter means that one price, adjusted to reflect transportation costs, must apply across all member countries.

Before the establishment of the European Union, countries had individual trade barriers to foster domestic agricultural industries. To some extent these trade barriers reflected the relative efficiency of various farming activities in different countries. The Netherlands was a low-cost dairy producer and Italy a high-cost dairy producer, this reflected differences in climate. Italy was a low-cost wine producer and Germany

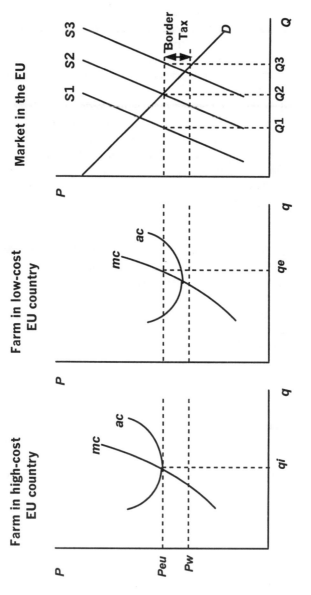

Figure 2.10: Evolution of the CAP

was a high-cost wine producer. With each country establishing its own trade barriers prior to the CAP, these differences in cost structure could be perpetuated. Thus, one could have a high-cost industry in one country and a low-cost industry in another country – the two stylized farms in Figure 2.10. Of course, within countries there would have been farms of different relative efficiency but we will abstract from that complication for ease of exposition.

Prior to the establishment of the CAP, Europe was a net importer of food. In the absence of any trade barriers imports would have been equal to the difference between $S1$ and D at the international price Pw. Of course, imports into Europe were never free but even with the existing trade barriers there were considerable imports. This was the period of the Cold War and western European security was at the top of the agenda of both European countries and the United States. Food security was a major issue with Europe under the threat of a Soviet submarine blockade. The memory of the breakdown in the European food system in the wake of the Second World War, resulting in widespread food shortages and hunger, was fresh in the minds of the populace and policy makers. Moving closer towards self-sufficiency seemed a reasonable goal for western European agriculture.

The European Economic Community (one of the precursors of the European Union) was established in part to strengthen western European economies against the Soviet threat. The CAP's trade policy reduced food import dependency and hence contributed to the broader security goal. As a result, the CAP's restrictions on foreign market access were accepted by the United States and other exporting countries as a cost that would have to be borne if Europe was to prosper.

To persuade individual countries to accept the CAP and its single price regime, common trade barriers had to be set high enough to support farms in the high-cost country for the particular commodity. Otherwise, high-cost farms would have been forced out of business by competition from more efficient members of the European Union – something that was politically unacceptable. Hence, trade barriers were imposed which effectively raised the within-EU price, Peu, above the international price, Pw, at a level where high-cost farms covered their costs at their chosen output, qi.

The short-run effects in the market were a decrease in imports to $Q2$ – $Q1$ helping to bring the European Union closer to self-sufficiency. Under this short-run analysis, the CAP appeared to satisfy the political requirement to support farmers in high-cost countries and to contribute to the wider security goal. Further, border tax revenues helped finance CAP rural adjustment initiatives. The market was not in equilibrium, however, and long-term forces were set in motion.

The high CAP prices meant that farmers in low-cost countries were making super-normal profits (*Peu* > *ac* at *qe*). Over time, the existence of these super-normal profits led to re-investment and encouraged entry. In turn, output increased, leading to a shift out in the supply curve. Of course, not all of the increase in supply can be attributed to the CAP; technological improvements would also have been increasing supply. However, in the space of 20 years, in commodity after commodity, the European Union went from being a net importer to being, first self-sufficient (*S2* = *D* at *Peu*) and then into surplus as supply (*S3*) exceeded demand at *Peu*.

Initially the surpluses, (*Q3* − *Q2*) were stored but their chronic nature soon led to the much-publicized butter and beef mountains, wine lakes and so on. Storage could only be an interim solution. Eventually, the surpluses had to be exported on to the international market under subsidy. The budgetary cost equalled *Peu* − *Pw* on each unit exported.

The size of the surpluses continued to expand because super-normal profits continued to exist in low-cost countries, encouraging evermore re-investment and entry, further shifting the supply curve to the right. Budgetary expenditures continued to expand, both because the size of the surpluses increased and because the large quantities forced on to the international market depressed the international price, increasing the gap between *Peu* and *Pw*. The increasing international market share of subsidized EU exports eventually led the United States to attempt to defend its traditional market share through its own subsidy programmes, perpetrating a virtual trade war between the United States and the European Union.

Tables 2.2, 2.3 and 2.4 support this stylized version of the evolution of the CAP. By 1979–80, EU prices were consistently above world market prices for a wide range of agricultural products (Table 2.2). EU and international prices increasingly diverged into the early 1990s, reflecting in part the downward pressure on international prices caused by increased EU exports. These high EU prices led in turn to the European Union moving from being a net importer to self-sufficiency and then to a net export position (Table 2.3). The size of the surpluses continued to increase through the 1980s. These surpluses were increasingly disposed of through subsidized exports, reflected in the increasing share of EU exports in international markets (Table 2.4).

Over time, the benefits brought by the CAP trade policy regime to farmers in low-cost countries were progressively capitalized into land values, driving the costs to new entrants up (shifting *ac* for low-cost farms up in Figure 2.10 until only normal profits remain). Eventually this capitalization reduces the incentive to enter and re-invest slowing the shift out in the short-run supply curve. The history of the CAP in the 1980s and early 1990s reflects attempts to manage this long-run disequilibrium. It also points to why CAP reform is so difficult. Reducing prices in the European Union would mean that farmers in high-cost countries would still face

Table 2.2 Ratio of EU prices to world prices, 1973–94

Product	1973–74	1979–80	1993–94
Common wheat	79	163	175
Durum wheat	116	159	167
Rice	60	131	140
Barley	96	161	168
Corn (maize)	98	190	200
Sugar	66	131	152
Beef and veal	110	204	177
Pork	131	152	147
Butter	320	411	485
Skimmed milk	156	379	400
Olive oil	96	193	185
Oilseeds	77	185	170

Source: European Commission, *The Agricultural Situation in the European Community* (various issues).

Table 2.3 EU self-sufficiency ratios, 1973–93

Product	1973	1983	1993
Cereals (excluding rice)	91	105	106
Sugar	90	123	130
Beef and veal	95	105	102
Pork	100	102	105
Butter	98	147	155
Cheese	103	107	109
Poultry meat	102	111	110

Source: European Commission, *Agricultural Statistics* (various issues).

Table 2.4 EU share of world exports, 1974 and 1984 (%)

Product	1974	1984	Change
Wheat	8.0	14.0	75
Corn (maize)	1.3	3.2	146
Total cereals (excluding rice)	6.0	10.0	67
Beef and veal	7.8	19.6	151
Poultry meat	5.6	23.6	321
Butter/butter oil	28.3	50.0	77
Cheese	37.8	53.2	41
Olive oil	4.0	21.0	425
Raw sugar	5.1	15.4	202
Raw tobacco	2.6	10.2	242
Citrus fruit	4.5	9.0	100
Apples	7.7	14.0	82

Source: United Nations, *Commodity Trade Statistics* (various issues).

bankruptcy. Further, as new entrants now have high costs due to capitalization, a considerable number of farmers in once low-cost countries also face financial hardship if prices are lowered. Lower levels of support mean reduced asset values, which threatens the viability of financial institutions. Other vested interests in the continuation of the CAP have also been created. The agro-input and processing industries have expanded to support surplus production ($Q3 - Q2$); reforms which would result in the downsizing of primary agriculture would put their investments at risk.

The long-run expansion of the agricultural sector and the capitalization of trade policy benefits are the fundamental reason why the European Union will continue to resist stricter WTO disciplines on export subsidies, domestic measures of support and access to its markets. It also explains why aggregate levels of support have not decreased as Uruguay Round reforms have taken place and the European Union has moved to more direct support of farmers.

2.8   MODELLING FOR AGRICULTURAL NEGOTIATIONS

A methodology for empirically implementing the partial equilibrium trade model is explored in this section. We begin by listing the informational requirements. We then show how to calculate the price and quantity effects, and, finally, we examine how to assess the impact on the economic welfare of consumers, producers, government and the country as a whole. Throughout the analysis, we will assume that the market in question is competitive.

We assume that, for a particular commodity, information is available on the (physical) quantities of domestic output, $Qs0$; consumption, $Qd0$; exports, $Xp0$; and imports, $Mp0$. (Similar calculations to those shown below could be made using value rather than physical data.) For seasonal reasons, for geographic reasons relating to transport and transaction costs, or for data-aggregation reasons, a country will often both export and import the same commodity. Initial output minus initial consumption yields initial net imports, $NX0$. Net exports are also equal to exports minus imports. Of course, negative net exports are simply positive net imports:

$$NX0 = Qs0 - Qd0 = X0 - M0.$$

In practice, this equation often provides an indirect route for calculating consumption from data on production and trade. For many agricultural products, adjustments in stocks and inventories typically arise. Since the modelling of inventories and adjustments in biological capital is difficult, we simply adjust initial consumption, which consists of demand by consumers, to include changes in stocks over the preceding year, which reflect demand by producers and/or government agencies.

We also need initial information on prices and/or government policy measures such as tariffs, export subsidies and production subsidies. A wide variety of policy measures have the potential to cause differences between world or border prices, Pw, demand or consumer prices, Pd, and supply or producer prices, Ps. Demand prices are equal to world prices plus trade measures, TM, plus consumption measures, CM:

$$Pd0 = Pw0 + TM0 + CM0.$$

Supply prices are equal to world prices plus trade measures plus production measures, PM, or to demand prices minus consumption measures plus production measures:

$$Ps0 = Pw0 + TM0 + PM0,$$

$$Ps0 = Pd0 - CM0 + PM0.$$

If there are no policy measures initially in place, the supply, demand and world prices would all be equal.

In this formulation, tariffs and export subsidies are positive trade-related measures that raise domestic (supply and demand) prices above the world price. Support or floor prices that apply to both producers and consumers and non-tariff barriers such as tariff rate quotas are other examples of positive trade-related measures. Export taxes or import subsidies would be negative trade measures, since they would push domestic (supply and demand) prices below the world price. Positive consumption measures include general or selective taxes that apply to the commodity in question and thereby push the demand price (further) above the world price. A consumption subsidy would be a negative consumption measure. A production subsidy is a positive production measure that raises the supply price (further) above the world price. An intervention price or floor price that applies only to producers is another example of a positive production measure, while a production tax would be a negative production measure. While consumption measures tend to be less important in agriculture, production measures, as well as trade measures, are very important. Production or domestic support measures are discussed in detail in Sections 3.7 and 3.8.

It is clearly necessary to have information on any changes in trade, consumption and production measures (that is, ΔTM, ΔCM and ΔPM) to carry out policy analysis. Changes in the domestic demand and supply prices will arise directly or indirectly from changes in policy measures:

$$\Delta Pd = \Delta TM + \Delta CM, \qquad Pd1 = Pd0 + \Delta Pd;$$

$$\Delta Ps = \Delta TM + \Delta PM, \qquad Ps1 = Ps0 + \Delta Ps.$$

The model can easily be adapted to allow for induced changes in the world price.

For simplicity, we will assume that the demand and supply curves are linear at least in the vicinity of the initial equilibrium. In order to extrapolate the linear demand and supply functions, it is necessary to have point estimates of the elasticities of demand and supply, εd and εs. These elasticities, which are ordinarily furnished by econometric studies, measure the proportionate quantity response to a small price change. More specifically, the elasticity of demand (supply) measures the percentage change in the quantity demanded (supplied) relative to the percentage change in the demand (supply) price. Demand or supply is said to be: (i) elastic if the percentage change in quantity exceeds the percentage change in price (that is, $\varepsilon d > 1$ or $\varepsilon s > 1$), (ii) unit elastic if the percentage changes in quantity and price are equal (that is, $\varepsilon d = 1$ or $\varepsilon s = 1$), or (iii) inelastic if the percentage change in quantity is less than the percentage change in price (that is, $\varepsilon d < 1$ or $\varepsilon s < 1$).[12] In Section 2.5, we differentiated between the short run and the long run. In the long run, adjustment constraints are irrelevant and the supply response to a price change is larger. Thus, long-run elasticities of supply, which are notoriously hard for economists to estimate, are larger or more elastic than short-run elasticities.

The elasticities of demand and supply are central to the calculation of the respective changes in consumption and output that arise from policy changes:

$$\Delta Qd = -\left(\frac{Qd0}{Pd0}\right) \times \varepsilon d \times \Delta Pd, \qquad Qd1 = Qd0 + \Delta Qd;$$

$$\Delta Qs = -\left(\frac{Qd0}{Pd0}\right) \times \varepsilon s \times \Delta Ps, \qquad Qs1 = Qs0 + \Delta Qs;$$

The changes in consumption and output are shown in panels (a) and (b) respectively in Figure 2.1. On the basis of these changes, we can also calculate the change in net exports:

$$\Delta NX = \Delta Qs - \Delta Qd, \qquad NX1 = NX0 + \Delta NX.$$

Increases in the demand price raise net exports (or lower net imports) by reducing consumption while increases in the supply price raise net exports by increasing output.

The impact of policy measures on the initial and final budgetary position of the government is central to the analysis. In either the initial or final state, net government revenue, GR, is equal to revenue from consumption measures, minus outlays on production measures, minus outlays on trade measures:

$$GR0 = (CM0 \times Qd0) - (PM0 \times Qs0) - (TM0 \times NX0);$$

$$GR1 = (CM1 \times Qd1) - (PM1 \times Qs1) - (TM1 \times NX1).$$

Revenue from consumption measures is positive if and only if the consumption measures are positive, and outlays on production measures are positive if and only if the production measures are positive. Outlays on trade measures are positive if the country is on a net export basis and its trade measures are positive (for example, exporting with export subsidies) or if it is on a net import basis and its trade measures are negative (for example, importing with import subsidies). Conversely, revenue is obtained from trade measures and outlays are negative whenever the country is on a net export basis and its trade measures are negative (for example, exporting with export taxes) or if it is on a net import basis and its trade measures are negative (for example, importing with tariffs).

The change in net government revenue, *GR*, is the first component of the assessment of the impact of policy changes on economic welfare:

$$\Delta GR = GR1 - GR0.$$

This government budget analysis is readily adapted to situations where a country adjusts its policy measures to conform to a regional trade that has common trade and/or domestic policies. For example, if a country such as Poland joined the European Union and harmonized with the CAP, it would lose its initial net revenue (or escape from its initial net outlays), while the European Union would gain the final net revenue (or lose the final net outlays).[13]

The change in consumer surplus corresponds to the loss of *b* + *c* dollars in panel (a) of Figure 2.1, and the change in producer surplus corresponds to a gain of *z* dollars in panel (b):

$$\Delta CS = \Delta Pd \times Qd0 \times \left[1 - 0.5 \times \varepsilon d \times \left(\frac{\Delta Pd}{Pd0}\right)\right]$$

$$\Delta PS = \Delta Ps \times Qs0 \times \left[1 - 0.5 \times \varepsilon s \times \left(\frac{\Delta Ps}{Ps0}\right)\right]$$

Increases in the relevant price raise the producer surplus but reduce the consumer surplus. In the short run, the producer surplus accrues primarily or entirely to producers *per se*, but in the long run it accrues entirely as rents to factors (such as land) that the industry uses intensively.

The one-period change in overall welfare or total surplus is equal to the sum of the changes in net government revenue, consumer surplus and producer surplus:

$$\Delta TS = \Delta GR + \Delta CS + \Delta PS.$$

Whatever the overall impact of the policy change, there are likely to be winners and losers. In particular, if the demand and supply prices move in the same direction, the interests of consumers and producers will be opposed.

We examine the cost of EU beef protection as a numerical example. In 1996, the European Union used an intervention or floor price of 3475 European Currency Units (ECU) per tonne, which was equivalent to US$4411 per tonne (OECD, 1998, p. 79). Based on OECD measures of (trade-related) market price support of 102 per cent, we can infer a world price of US$2184 per tonne.[14] Export subsidies and tariff rate quotas (TRQs) were used as auxiliary measures to keep the EU floor price above the world price. For simplicity, we assume that headage and other domestic support measures remain unchanged. The net output of beef by the European Union was 7.95 million tonnes in 1996, and net exports were 0.708 million tonnes (European Commission, 1997).[15] Thus it can be inferred that EU consumption was 7.242 million tonnes.

The removal of EU market price support would have generated an increase in consumption to 10.35 million tonnes assuming an elasticity of demand of 0.85. Elasticities of supply are highly time-sensitive so we examine cases where the elasticity takes on values of· 0.2 and 1.5. Interpreting these as short- and long-run elasticities, EU output would have fallen somewhat to 7.147 million tonnes in the short run and would have fallen precipitously to 1.929 million tonnes in the long run. In the short run the European Union would have switched away from exporting and would have imported 3.203 million tonnes. In the long run, imports would have risen dramatically to 8.42 million tonnes.

The removal of trade-related support measures would have increased the consumer surplus by US$19.589 billion per annum. In the short run, producer surplus would have fallen by US$16.811 billion. Long-run rents on inputs used intensively in beef production would eventually fall by US$11.001 billion per year. Since these rents originally would have been capitalized into agricultural assets such as land, there would be very sizeable capital losses on such assets. This would certainly precipitate bankruptcies for producers carrying significant debt loads, even if they were efficient. The budgetary saving to the European Union from the removal of export subsidies would have been US$1.577 billion per annum.[16] In the initial year the efficiency gain or increase in total surplus would have been US$4.354 billion. The efficiency gain would eventually approach US$10.165 billion per annum in the long run after adjustment costs diminished.

NOTES

1. An interesting CGE model is presented by Hertel, Brockmeier and Swaminathan (1997). This model is restricted to ten commodities, only four of which are food-related. The model also considers groups of central and eastern European countries rather than individual countries. Thus divergent trade policy measures get averaged across countries as well as sectors. This obscuring of market detail is very typical in CGE models. Thus the incorporation of general equilibrium linkages between markets comes at a real cost.

2. The final expenditure on pork will be less than or greater than the initial expenditure depending on whether the percentage reduction in the quantity demanded is less than or greater than the percentage increase in price. In the former case, where the percentage reduction in the quantity demanded is less than the percentage increase in price, demand is said to be inelastic, while in the latter case it is said to be elastic.

3. The assessment of changes in consumer surplus becomes somewhat more complicated if policy measures force consumption to take place off the demand curve.

4. In our discussion we assume that Japan initially pursued a policy of free trade. In actual fact, however, Japan recently converted a system of quantitative restrictions on rice imports to tariffs at a rate of US$2680 per tonne (OECD, 1999, p. 42).

5. Equivalent overall gains from trade arise for Poland in the beef market depicted in Figure 2.4. Under free trade at a world price of Pw, $Qs0 - Qd0$ gives exports. The price increase from Pa to Pw benefits producers by generating an increase in producer surplus equal to areas $z1 + z2 + z3 + z4$. Consumers are harmed by the loss of consumer surplus equal to area $z1 + z2 + z3$. While producers win and consumers lose, there is an overall gain to Poland of $z4$.

6. Such gains would be a certainty if the economy consisted entirely of competitive markets of the type being considered here.

7. An equivalent analysis applies to Polish wheat imports in Figure 2.3. The reduction in price from Pa to Pw leads to imports of $Qd0 - Qs0$. Producer surplus declines by areas $z1 + a1$, but consumer surplus rises by areas $z1 + z2 + z3 + a1 + ... + a5$. Thus, there is an unambiguous gain in total surplus to Poland from introducing free trade equal to $z2 + z3 + a2 + ... + a5$.

8. The percentage response in quantity demanded to a small percentage increase in income is formally known as the product's income elasticity of demand. For most food products and other necessities, income elasticities are low.

9. If the expansion of the industry as a whole bids up the price of one or more variable input, the industry is said to face increasing costs. In this case, the short-run supply curve will be steeper than the simple horizontal sum of the supply curves of the individual firms. As we will see, industries are much more likely to face increasing costs in the long run when all inputs or factors of production can be varied.

10. As industry output increases, the value of underlying inputs such as land may be bid up. In this case, at least part of the producer surplus will accrue in the form of higher rents on land. As we will see, such increasing costs are more prevalent in the long run.

11. As we will discuss further in Chapter 3, if an asset is expected to generate a flow of net earnings of B for T years at a discount or interest rate of r, its purchase price or net present value will be:

$$NPV = \sum_{i=1}^{T} \frac{B}{(1+r)^i}$$

Thus if a milk quota is expected to generate annual rents of 100 000 for five years when the interest rate is 5 per cent, the purchase price of the quota will be: 100 000.00 + 95 238.10 + 90 702.95 + 86 383.76 + 82 270.24 = US$454 495.05. If the asset is expected to generate a perpetual flow of earnings, its net present value will be: NPV = B/r. Thus, if a milk quota is expected to generate annual rents of US$100 000 forever with the interest rate at 5 per cent, the purchase price of the quota will be: US$2 000 000.

12. It can be shown that the elasticity of demand (supply) is equal to the ratio of the quantity demanded (supplied) to the demand (supply) price divided by the slope of the demand (supply) curve.

13. While Poland would make an overall contribution to the EU budget, this would be independent of the budgetary transfers on any and all markets.

14. The OECD's consumer nominal assistance coefficient (NAC) provides a measure of market price support and consumer subsidies with the latter being negligible for EU beef. The consumer NAC was reported as 2.02 (OECD, 1998, p. 76).

15. In fact, the European Union exported 1.104 million tonnes of beef and imported 0.395 million tonnes. In this case, the key reason for simultaneous imports and exports was the market support policy itself. Nevertheless, it is not unusual for a country to both export and import the same commodity. This can happen for seasonal reasons, for geographic reasons relating to transport and transaction costs, or for data aggregation reasons.

16. This calculation omits savings in administrative costs relating to export subsidies and TRQs.

3. Unfinished business

3.1 TRADE BARRIERS: TARIFFS, IMPORT QUOTAS AND TARIFF RATE QUOTAS

There is a wide assortment of non-tariff barriers (NTBs) that are similar to tariffs in that they reduce imports. Prior to the Uruguay Round, the agricultural sector was largely excluded from the general GATT provisions on tariffication and tariff reduction. Consequently, NTBs such as import quotas (pre-announced quantitative limits on imports) and variable levies (border taxes that increase or decrease to adjust protection to changes in world prices) were prominent in agriculture. In moving agriculture into closer conformity with the rest of the GATT, the Uruguay Round Agreement on Agriculture (URAA) required the conversion of all NTBs to tariff-rate quotas (TRQs) or directly to tariffs. The continuance of import quotas on rice was permitted for Japan, Korea and the Philippines, and Israel was allowed to retain import quotas on sheep meat and cheese. Nevertheless, in 1999 Japan elected to convert its rice quota to a tariff (OECD, 1999, p. 124). Further, the URAA specified that all agricultural tariffs, including the new TRQs were to be subject to negotiated reductions over the five-year period to 1999. The developed countries committed to a 36 per cent reduction overall, and a minimum 15 per cent reduction on each commodity, while developing countries committed to a 20 per cent reduction overall and a 10 per cent reduction on each commodity. No reductions were required of the least developed countries.[1]

The analysis of tariffs in the previous chapter has shown that tariffs restrict trade and protect the domestic market by raising the home market price. Such protection benefits producers at the expense of consumers. If the world price remains unchanged, there is an overall welfare loss because the gains in producer surplus and government revenue are insufficient to offset the decline in consumer surplus. Most NTBs have broadly similar effects. In this chapter, we begin by focusing on import quotas and then we turn to TRQs.

Import quotas are quantitative restrictions on imports that place an upper bound on the amount that can be imported. Import licences are often, but not always, used to implement the system of import quotas and provide traders with a degree of certainty that any shipments that are made will be accepted at the border. In Figure 3.1, the quantity of imports, which is given by the difference between the quantities demanded and supplied on the domestic market, would be equal to $Qd0 - Qs0$ in the absence of any barriers to trade. Now suppose that an import quota is introduced such that the quantity of imports is constrained to be no larger than the quota, which is shown. The quota limits on imports given by the distance between the vertical lines pushes the domestic or home market price above the world price, to Pd. While the increase in the domestic price is beneficial to producers, it is more costly to consumers. In particular, the gain in producer surplus is only $a1$ dollars whereas the loss in consumer surplus is $a1 + \ldots + a4$ dollars.

Each import licence generates rents, since it entitles the holder to buy a unit of product at Pw and sell it at Pd. Thus, the one-period value of the import license is $Pd - Pw$, and the aggregate value of all licences is $a3$ dollars. Given the presence of these 'trade restriction rents' of $a3$ dollars, we can calculate the change in total surplus on this market to be an efficiency loss of $a2 + a4$ dollars. A comparison of Figure 3.1 with Figure 2.3 reveals broad similarities between the import quota and an import tariff. In fact, at the level of analysis shown in Figure 3.1, if a tariff were used to raise the domestic price to Pd, the only apparent difference would be that the trade restriction rents of $a3$ dollars would accrue as tariff revenue. We discuss issues concerning trade-restriction rents in detail in the following section.

In spite of the fact that import quotas and tariffs have broadly similar effects, they are not economically equivalent policies. Import quotas are potentially inconsistent with the general GATT principles of transparency and non-discrimination. At a minimum, traders are encumbered with additional transaction costs to acquire import licences prior to shipment. Further, the import licences may be arbitrarily allocated among countries and/or firms so that imports may originate with inefficient producers. In the presence of economic growth, import quotas are also more restrictive and inefficient than tariffs. Tariffs, unlike import quotas, permit increases in trade volumes as import demand and/or export supplies rise. For similar reasons, import quotas are more inefficient than tariffs in the presence of

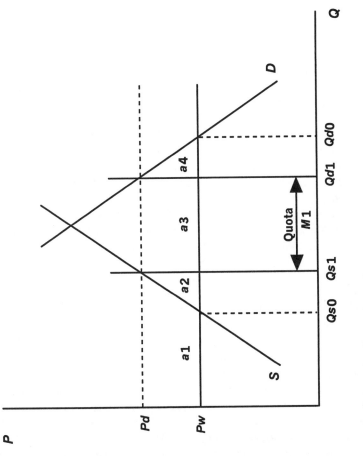

Figure 3.1: An import quota

imperfect competition. For example, if there is a single domestic firm or marketing board, it can raise its price with impunity if there is an import quota because additional imports cannot rush in in response to monopolistic pricing practices. For any given volume of imports, therefore, an import quota leads to a higher domestic price than a tariff because there is no threat of additional competition from imports. In view of this, it is hardly surprising that prior to the Uruguay Round Canada used import quotas to buttress its system of marketing boards and supply management in the poultry, egg and dairy sectors.

If the world price tends to vary more than domestic demand and supply, an import quota would keep the domestic price more stable than a tariff. Where the stabilization of a domestic price is a trade policy goal, however, a variable levy is a much more effective instrument. A variable levy is a tariff that varies to exactly offset fluctuations in the world price and maintain a constant price in the home market. In an environment of declining world prices for food driven by technological change, however, variable levies become increasingly protectionist. They were formerly used extensively under the European Union's Common Agricultural Policy.

Tariff rate quotas (TRQs), or tariff quotas (TQs) as they are sometimes called, represent another type of import measure. In the agricultural sector, TRQs gained new prominence at the conclusion of the Uruguay Round as a transition measure from import quotas, variable levies and other NTBs towards tariffs. TRQs are essentially a hybrid of import quotas and tariffs. All imports up to a quantity limit on preferred access to the domestic market known as the 'TRQ-quota' are subject to a low 'within-quota tariff', while any additional imports are subject to a higher 'above-quota tariff'. In some cases, the within-quota tariff may be set equal to zero.

Under a TRQ, imports may be limited by the above-quota tariff, the TRQ quota or the within-quota tariff. In Figure 3.2, imports are limited by the above-quota tariff, AQT. This is particularly transparent in Panel (b), which shows the import demand curve, MD. In this figure, the domestic price, Pd, is equal to the world price, Pw, plus the above-quota tariff. Domestic consumption under the TRQ is at $Qd1$, domestic production is at $Qs1$, and total imports are $Qd1 - Qs1$. The TRQ-quota allows the first MQ units of imports to enter the domestic market at the within-quota tariff of WQT, but the remainder enters at the above-quota tariff.

The TRQ-induced increase in the domestic price leads to an increase in producer surplus of $a1 + b1$ dollars and a reduction in consumer surplus of $a1 + ... + a5 + b1 + ... b5$ dollars. The government collects $b3$ dollars in revenue from the within-quota tariff and $a4 + b4$ dollars from the above-

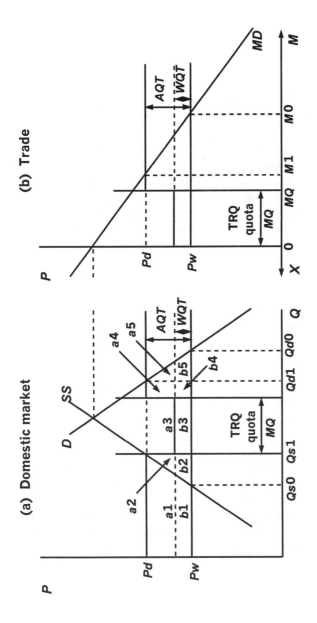

Figure 3.2: A tariff rate quota (TRQ)

71

tariff quota. There is an additional $a3$ dollars of trade restriction rents that accrue to the holders of import licences since they can purchase at Pw on the world market, pay the within-quota tariff of WQT and then sell at Pd. Consequently, there is a loss in total surplus of $a2 + b2 + a5 + b5$ dollars. This represents the efficiency loss attributable to the TRQ. It should be observed that TRQs, like import quotas, are less transparent and more likely to be discriminatory than pure tariffs. Firms face additional transaction costs to acquire import licences, and the licences may be arbitrarily allocated among countries or firms. While TRQs are superior to import quotas in accommodating economic growth, they provide more shelter than tariffs to domestic firms and marketing agencies that have market power.

Figure 3.3 shows various import demand situations. If the applicable import demand curve is $MD5$, imports are limited by the above-quota tariff just as they were in Figure 3.2. In this case, the domestic price is equal to $Pw + AQT$. The 'fill rate', or proportion of the TRQ quota being utilized, is 100 per cent, and additional imports enter at the above-tariff quota. If the import demand curve happens to be $MD3$, however, imports are limited by the TRQ quota and the domestic price is $Pd3$. While the fill rate is still 100 per cent, there are no above-quota imports and the above-quota tariff is non-constraining in the sense that it has no effect on imports. Now suppose that $MD1$ represents the import demand curve. The total imports of $M1$ are now limited by the within-quota tariff. The fill rate is less than 100 per cent and the domestic price is equal to $Pw + WQT$. Both the TRQ-quota and the above-quota tariff are non-constraining. If the import demand curve happens to be $MD4$, the TRQ quota is constraining on imports and the above-quota tariff is on the verge of being constraining. If the import demand curve is $MD2$, the within-quota tariff is constraining and the TRQ quota is on the verge of being constraining. With both $MD2$ and $MD4$, like $MD3$, the fill rate is 100 per cent and there are no above-quota imports. Finally, if the relevant import demand curve is $MD0$, there would be no imports under the TRQ; the within-quota tariff would be prohibitive.

Figure 3.3 can also be used to analyse the conversion from an import quota to an equivalent TRQ. Suppose that the import demand curve is $MD3$ and the initial import quota was equal to MQ. In this case, the initial domestic price was $Pd3$. Provided that the within-quota tariff is set no greater than $Pd3 - Pw$ and the TRQ quota is set at MQ, access to the domestic market for imports will remain unchanged. The setting of an above-quota tariff does not matter for assuring equivalent minimum access. Even if the above-quota tariff is set at AQT in Figure 3.3, imports of MQ still enter the domestic market. By moving from import quotas to equal

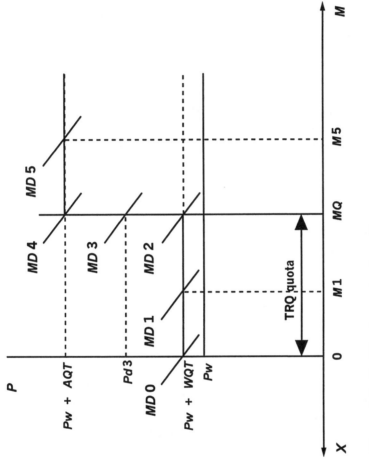

Figure 3.3: Tariff rate quotas in action

TRQ quotas, therefore, the Uruguay Round process guaranteed that tariffication could not be abused to the extent that there was less access for imports.

Suppose that, in addition, the above-quota tariff was set equal to $Pd3 - Pw$ so that it is just on the verge of being import constraining. Such was the intended outcome of the initial conversion from import quotas to TRQs. Now either a reduction in the above-quota tariff or an increase in the TRQ-quota will improve access for foreign exporters. The setting of the above-tariff quota, while unimportant from the standpoint of maintaining access, is very important from the standpoint of increasing access and providing further trade liberalization. It would seem that many countries engaged in 'dirty tariffication', and set their above-quota tariffs much higher (for example, at AQT) so that the subsequent tariff cuts agreed under the URAA, would be completely ineffective. Podbury and Roberts (1999, p. 2) point out that

> [t]his 'water in the tariffs' means that relatively large reductions in some bound tariffs might have little actual effect on market access. That increases the importance of achieving reductions in bound rates that are sufficient to reduce actual rates. It also highlights the important role that provision of minimum access and assurance of current access will need to continue to play in the coming negotiations.

Issues concerning the negotiations on access will be developed further in Section 3.3.

In surprisingly many cases, fill rates have turned out to be less than 100 per cent so that even the TRQ-quota is not import constraining. One possible explanation is that the improvements in access have been so dramatic that the TRQ-quotas are no longer import constraining. Unfortunately, in many instances such an optimistic appraisal is rather naïve. Another explanation of observed fill rates of less than 100 per cent involves abnormal market conditions. Suppose that the expected import demand curve is $MD4$ (or $MD3$) in Figure 3.3. If domestic supply is unusually high or domestic demand is unusually low, the import demand curve that is realized may be $MD1$ and the fill rate may be less than 100 per cent. An unusually high world price could also choke off imports and result in a fill rate of less than 100 per cent. Of course, if domestic demand is unusually high or supply is unusually low, import demand might be given by $MD5$ leading to above-quota imports. Another reason that fill rates may be less than 100 per cent involves the transaction costs of obtaining import licences. These costs will depend on the administration procedures for the

TRQ. Various methods of administering TRQs are considered in the next section.

3.2 VALUABLE TRADING RIGHTS AND THEIR CONTROL

Of course, any 'right' that allows a firm to earn economic rents will have value. Any trade-restricting regime will create trade-restriction rents and, thus, valuable trading rights. This is true not only for import-restricting regimes such as tariffs, TRQs and import quotas, but also for export-restricting regimes such as export taxes and voluntary export restraints (VERs). These valuable trading rights arise because there is a favourable wedge between prices in the world and in the domestic market. For example, consider a case where imports into the domestic market are limited and the domestic price exceeds the world price. Since the price at which imports can be acquired in the international market is less than the price at which they can be sold in the importing country, an opportunity to benefit from the price divergence is created. The opportunity will be realized by the party that acquires the right to capture that price differential. If exports from a domestic market are restricted such that the domestic price is below the world price, there is a similar opportunity.

To begin with, we explore six possible ways to assign valued trading rights. In two cases, the rights can be assigned to private firms. In the other four cases the right is assigned to the government of either the importing or the exporting country. We then turn explicitly to TRQs where the government of the importing country may share the trade restriction rents with other parties. Other cases where the trade restriction rents are shared between the governments and between governments and private firms are also possible but we do not explore them here. We look explicitly at the case where imports to the domestic market are to be restricted, but the analysis is analogous for the case where exports are restricted.

The six cases can be explored using Figure 3.1. Assume that a trade policy is implemented that limits imports to $Qd1 - Qs1$ or $M1$. This means that goods can be acquired in the international market at Pw and sold at Pd. A monetary value equal to area $a3$ can be captured by whoever is assigned the right to exploit it. This 'valued trading right' will be the subject of negotiation between countries. For example, trade could be limited through a quantitative restriction on the amount traded. This could be accomplished either by the exporting country imposing a VER that limits its exports to $M1$ or by the importing country imposing an import quota equal to $M1$.

First, consider the two cases where the valued import rights are assigned to firms. If the importing country imposes an import quota, it will be faced with excess demand for imports above the quantity of the import quota. It will then have to allocate the right to import among its firms. If it simply divides the right among its firms at no cost to the firms, each firm will benefit by the amount $Pd - Pw$ times the quantity it is allowed to import. In total, importing firms will benefit by area $a3$ because they can buy at Pw but sell at Pd. If the right is distributed over a number of production periods, as with any policy-induced profit opportunity it will become capitalized over the length of the period for which the right has been allocated.

In practice there are a number of methods of assigning these trading rights to firms. Some procedures are relatively transparent. For example, import licences can be assigned on a historic basis, a first-come, first-served basis, or a licence-on-demand basis. In a licence-on-demand system, firms request licences. If the aggregate requests are less than the import quota, licences are issued accordingly, but if the aggregate requests exceed the quota all requests are reduced proportionally. There are also procedures that are less transparent. For example, import licences could be allocated by either producer organizations or state trading agencies. Combinations of procedures may also be used, as when trading rights are allocated to countries on a historic basis and then to firms on a first-come, first-served basis. All of these methods of allocating trading rights can be classified as non-market administration procedures. While firms may face administrative fees in acquiring import licences, they do not pay for the full value of the right that they receive.

Alternatively, suppose that the exporting country voluntarily agrees to restrict its exports to $M1$. It will have firms wishing to supply more exports than the restricted amount, $M1$. If quantity is simply allocated at no cost among exporting firms, then in aggregate the exporting firms will benefit by the value $a3$ – again because they can buy at Pw and sell at Pd. Whenever private firms receive the right to export or import, therefore, the benefit of the trade restriction rents accrues to the firms in question.

Consider next the two cases where governments auction·valued trading rights to firms. As the trading rights have value to the firms, they will be willing to pay to acquire them. In the case of an import quota, the importing country could auction the right to the highest bidder. In this case, revenues equal to $a3$ accrue to the importing country's treasury and could be used for investments in rural restructuring or technological improvement. Auctioning is clearly a market-based allocation mechanism, and it has the added advantage that imports will be sourced from the most cost-efficient firms that can offer product on the most competitive terms. This is because they can afford to out bid less efficient firms at the quota auction. By contrast, the non-market mechanisms considered above will not ensure that imports come from the most efficient firms. Thus, the non-market mechanisms entail an additional efficiency loss over and above the loss attributable to trade restriction *per se* (for example, in addition to $a2 + a4$ dollars). Auctioning the trading rights has the additional advantage that it is self-rationing. This eliminates the need to allocate bureaucratically among competing interests and removes opportunities for corruption and the incentive to engage in rent-seeking activities. In a similar fashion, if the exporting country institutes a VER, the right to export could be auctioned; revenue $a3$ would then accrue to the exporting country's treasury.

The final two alternatives relate to direct taxation of the right by the importing or exporting country. The importing country can tax the right by imposing a tariff. Revenue $a3$ accrues to the importing country's treasury. As exports are based on cost plus tariff, this means that the lowest cost firm (the most efficient firm) will be the one to supply the export market. In comparison with auctions of import licences, tariffs are likely to save on transaction costs. Revenue of $a3$ dollars, alternatively, could be captured by the exporting country if it were to impose an export tax.

The trade restriction rents generated by TRQs are somewhat more complex. In Figure 3.2, the within-quota tariff, WQT, yielded government revenue of $b3$ dollars and the above-quota tariff, AQT, yielded $a4 + b4$ dollars. Licences eligible to import under the within-tariff quota represent a valuable trading right, because product can be bought at the world price, Pw, and sold at the domestic price, Pd, after paying the within-quota tariff. Thus, there are $a3$ dollars in additional trade restriction rents that can be auctioned or allocated to firms through any of the non-market mechanisms discussed above.

Interestingly enough, 646 of the world total of 1279 TRQs that had been notified to the WTO (that is, 50.5 per cent) were being administered on an applied tariff basis where all imports, regardless of the aggregate quantity, were permitted at the within-quota tariff (Skully, 1999, pp. 8–11). In other words, the TRQ-quota was simply being ignored. Administering a TRQ on an applied tariff basis affords a country extra flexibility. On any particular commodity, a country's 'bound' tariff is the maximum tariff consistent with its WTO obligations. Bound tariffs typically coincide with the above-quota tariff. Thus in an emergency, the country could afford its domestic producers additional protection by choosing to raise its tariff on above-quota product to the official above-quota tariff rate. Further, it could do so without the penalty of paying compensation or facing retaliation. Over half the TRQs that were being administered as applied tariffs were notified by just three countries: Norway (213), Poland (79) and Iceland (78) (Skully, 1999, Table 2). Both Norway and Iceland may wish to leave open the possibility of easy future entry into the European Union without the difficulty of having to raise trade barriers and pay compensation or face retaliation. The same consideration is even more immediate for Poland, which is currently negotiating accession to the European Union and will have to adopt the Common Agricultural Policy (CAP).

Of the remaining 633 WTO-notified TRQs that were being fully enforced, only 76 (12 per cent) were allocated exclusively by auction; the remaining 557 were assigned at least in part on a non-market basis (Skully, 1999, p. 9). On a world basis, licence on demand was the most prevalent form of non-market assignment mechanism (314), with first-come, first-served (104) a distant second. Historic assignments and assignments via producer groups or state trading agencies accounted for 30 TRQs each. Mixed methods (47), other methods (21) and unspecified methods (10) accounted for the remainder of TRQs (p. 9).

Skully (1999, Table 2) also reports that TRQ administration varies considerably across countries. The United States notified 54 TRQs to the WTO. Of these, 32 were assigned on a first-come, first-served basis, 17 were by mixed methods and five were not specified. Of the European Union's 85 TRQs, 58 were on a licence-on-demand basis, 20 were on a first-come, first-served basis, six were on a historic basis and one was by mixed methods. Japan had 20 TRQs. Of these, 13 were on a licence-on-demand basis, four were allocated by state trading agencies, one was allocated by mixed methods and two were allocated by other methods.

The prevalence of non-market administration methods for TRQs poses additional considerations that may be raised in connection with the WTO negotiations on market access. We turn next to issues concerning the WTO negotiations on market access.

3.3 IMPROVING ACCESS BY ADJUSTING TARIFF RATE QUOTAS

Since the general WTO rules permit only tariff barriers, TRQs must eventually be eliminated. One possible outcome of the current set of negotiations would be to complete the conversion of TRQs into tariffs. While this outcome may be rather unlikely, it has much to recommend it. In this section, we begin by considering such a complete conversion. Thereafter, we examine more limited improvements to market access that liberalize trade in the context of TRQs and that may also reform TRQ administration.

Suppose that the current round of negotiations led to the complete replacement of TRQs with tariffs. Before any steps are made to improve access, it is necessary to ask what tariff is equivalent to a TRQ. Not surprisingly, the equivalent tariff would generally lie between the within-quota tariff and the above-quota tariff. Precisely where between these limits the equivalent tariff would lie depends on the circumstances. Two cases are relatively straightforward. Where above-quota imports were typically observed under the TRQ regime, the equivalent tariff would be equal to the above-quota tariff. Where fill rates were typically less than 100 per cent under the TRQ regime, the equivalent tariff, neglecting transaction costs, would be equal to the within-quota tariff. While a small allowance might be made for transaction costs, it is very tempting to ignore these costs in calculating tariff equivalents as a punishment for countries that wilfully adopted inefficient and deceptive practices in TRQ administration.

Finding the tariff that is equivalent to a TRQ is more difficult when the fill rate is 100 per cent (that is, the TRQ-quota is import constraining) but there are no above-quota imports. Suppose that typical import demands are given by the $MD3$ curve in Figure 3.3. In this case, the equivalent per unit tariff would be equal to $Pd3 - Pw$. As we saw in Section 3.1, countries were supposed to determine the equivalent above-quota tariffs in this manner after the Uruguay Round. However, many countries seem to have set higher above-quota tariffs to partially renege on their Uruguay Round liberalization commitments. This has two implications. First, there may be many situations of this type to deal with in the current negotiations. Second, careful scrutiny is needed to make sure that countries set economically warranted equivalent tariffs. Of course, determining equivalent tariffs would only be the prerequisite to negotiations on tariff reduction.

Unfortunately, there may not be sufficient political will for full tariffication. Consequently, trade-liberalizing efforts will likely take place in a context where TRQs continue to be permissible. Here again thorny problems arise, since the liberalizing efforts could focus on expanding access under TRQ-quotas, reducing above-quota tariffs, or reducing or eliminating the within-quota tariffs. Figure 3.3 can be used to shed light on this issue.

If the import demand curve is *MD5*, a reduction in the above-quota tariff will serve to increase access, but a modest increase in the TRQ-quota will not increase imports. The TRQ-quota would have to increase beyond *M5* to have any effect. Of course, importing countries might be anxious to offer modest quantity concessions instead of tariff concessions on such markets. If there was a reduction in the above-quota tariff, it would lead to a decline in the domestic price. This would harm domestic producers but be beneficial for consumers. Tariff revenue could rise due to the increase in imports or fall due to the reduction in the tariff. Trade restriction rents on the TRQ-quota would fall due to the reduction in the domestic price. There would be an overall improvement in efficiency as trade distortions were reduced.

By contrast, if the import demand curve is *M3*, an increase in the TRQ-quota will increase imports but a modest reduction in the above-quota tariff will have no effect. The above-quota tariff would have to fall below $Pd3 - Pw$ in order to have any effect on imports. In such a situation, it would appear likely that importing countries would prefer to offer modest tariff concessions. If the TRQ-quota were increased, the domestic price would fall and once again cause a decline in producer surplus but an increase in consumer surplus and total surplus. Tariff revenue would be unchanged. While the per unit value of import licences would fall due to the reduction in the domestic price, the aggregate value of the trade restriction rents could rise due to the increase in within-quota imports.

When the import demand curve is *MD4*, either a cut in the above-quota tariff or an increase in the TRQ-quota will increase imports. If the import demand curve is *MD2*, however, an increase in the TRQ-quota is required; a reduction in the within-quota tariff will have no effect on imports. Finally, if the import demand curve is given by *MD1* (or, indeed, *MD0*), only a cut in the within-quota tariff will raise imports. Here, the importing country may well offer reductions in the above-quota tariffs and/or an increase in the TRQ-quota, neither of which will be effective.

A final issue arises with respect to TRQs that have been administered on an applied tariff basis where all imports are permitted at the within-quota tariff. On the one hand, it would be completely reasonable to negotiate reductions in within-quota tariffs as part of a deal on access. On the other hand, some agricultural exporting countries have advocated a reduction in bound tariffs to the applied within-quota tariff. This would effectively pre-convert such TRQs to tariffs. Since this would punish those countries that had gone beyond their Uruguay Round commitments, it seems manifestly unjust. Further, such a requirement would set an odious precedent for the future administration of trade policy. Many of the countries that administer TRQs on an applied tariff basis desire an extra degree of flexibility. Some countries anticipate needing this flexibility to ease their prospective entry into regional trade agreements that have common external barriers. For example, even though Poland administers a large proportion of its TRQs on an applied tariff basis, it will need to use the access provisions of those TRQs to reduce the compensation that is required upon accession to the European Union and adoption of the CAP. A similar issue arises with ordinary tariffs that are currently assessed at a rate below the bound tariff rate. Once again, it would be undesirable to punish countries that have gone beyond their previous commitments.

There has been some additional discussion on reforming TRQ administration, primarily among trade economists rather than policy makers. One suggestion would be to require TRQs to be administered through market mechanisms. This would require either the auctioning of licences to import at the within-quota tariff or administration as an applied tariff with all imports permitted at the within-quota tariff rate. Market-based TRQ administration would probably improve efficiency and transparency and lessen the possibility of discrimination across countries and/or firms. The inevitable downfall of any proposal for requiring market-based TRQ administration is that it completely removes distributive flexibility. This means that governments cannot help offset the impact of liberalization by conferring valuable trading rights on adversely affected parties. Of course, the lack of distributive flexibility has an important positive side as well since it greatly reduces the opportunities for corruption and the incentives for rent-seeking activities.

If a requirement for market-based TRQ administration is not likely to garner much support, is there any alternative reform that is more practicable? Skully (1999, p. 3) points out that it might be more politically tractable simply to require that all import licences be re-saleable. Such a requirement would generate significant efficiency improvements without compromising distributive flexibility. If the most efficient exporters did not obtain import licences in the initial distribution, it would be mutually advantageous for them to buy such licences from less efficient producers on the secondary market. Of course, the possibility of discrimination remains in spite of the efficiency improvement since it goes hand in hand with distributive flexibility. Nevertheless, a reform that required import licences to be fully tradable would significantly improve TRQ administration and would be most welcome.

Access issues are central to current WTO negotiations. The complexities of TRQ liberalization and administration guarantee that these negotiations will be very difficult. No doubt, formula-based approaches will be proposed. Due to both the inherent complexities of TRQs and the dirty tariffication after the Uruguay Round, all proposals will require careful evaluation.

3.4 CONTROLLING EXPORT SUBSIDIES AT THE WTO

At its inception, the GATT attempted to prohibit the use of export subsidies. However, an exception was made for agricultural and other primary products. Ironically, this exception came at the insistence of the United States. By the 1980s, world grain prices were being artificially depressed to a significant degree by the competitive export subsidies of major producing countries such as the European Union and the United States.

Reacting against these 'grain subsidy wars' in the Uruguay Round negotiations, the United States led the charge to try to eliminate agricultural export subsidies completely. This position was strongly supported by agricultural exporting countries, but staunchly resisted by the European Union, which advocated gradualism. The debate over agricultural export subsidies was both heated and protracted and the controversy threatened to undermine the whole of the negotiations. After this issue forced several extensions to the Uruguay Round, the gradualist position of the European Union ultimately triumphed to the extent that export subsidies were only reduced and not eliminated. The uneasy compromise represented by the URAA required that developed countries reduce their total outlays on agricultural export subsidies by 36 per cent over five years, and also reduce the volume of goods subject to export subsidies by 21 per cent. In developing countries, outlays on export subsidies had to be reduced by 20 per cent over ten years, and the volume of goods subject to export subsidies 14 per cent. For the European Union, however, this gradualism came at a price. The URAA pre-committed countries to start a new round of negotiations on further reductions to export subsidies in 2000.

To fully understand the problem of controlling export subsidies that confronts the current WTO negotiations, it is necessary to examine the impact on the world market of an exports subsidy imposed by a large trading entity such as the European Union or the United States. Figure 3.4 shows the situation where the European Union is an exporter of grain and the curve *Sx* represents its supply of grain to the world market (that is, net of its own demand). Since the European Union is large, its supply of grain to the world market has an impact on the world price. Thus the European Union faces a negatively sloped import demand curve from the rest of the world as a whole, given by *Dm**. This import demand curve represents the demand for grain net of supply in the rest of the world. If the European Union does not subsidize its grain exports, the world and the European price will be *P*1 euros per tonne and the quantity traded will be *X*1 tonnes.

Now, suppose that the European Union implements an export subsidy equal to *ES* euros. Notice that the height of *Dm** indicates the price that non-Europeans are willing to pay for each unit of grain purchased on the world market, while the height of the *Sx* curve indicates the price, inclusive of the export subsidy, that Europeans are willing to accept. In the post-subsidy equilibrium, the price in the European market, given by the *Sx* curve, exceeds the world price given by the *Dm** curve by exactly *ES* euros. Thus the export subsidy leads to an increase in grain exports from *X*1 to *X*2 tonnes, an increase in the EU home market price from *P*1 to *Ph*2, and a decline in the world price from *P*1 to *Pw*2. By considering the reduction in the world price caused by the increase in EU exports, this analysis goes a step beyond the small-country analysis shown in Figure 2.4 where the world price was assumed to be constant. In both the small and large country cases, an export subsidy increases the volume of exports, raises the home market price above the world price and thereby necessitates an auxiliary protective measure, such as a tariff or variable levy, to keep low-price products from entering or re-entering the domestic market. If the country is large enough to have a perceptible influence on the world price, then the world price will fall as a result of the increased supply on the world market.

The export subsidy results in a net private-sector gain for Europeans of *a* + *b* euros that we will call a gain in 'exporter surplus'. Since the European Union is on an export basis where output exceeds consumption, the magnitude of the gain in producer surplus from the higher European price unambiguously exceeds the loss in consumer surplus and gives rise to

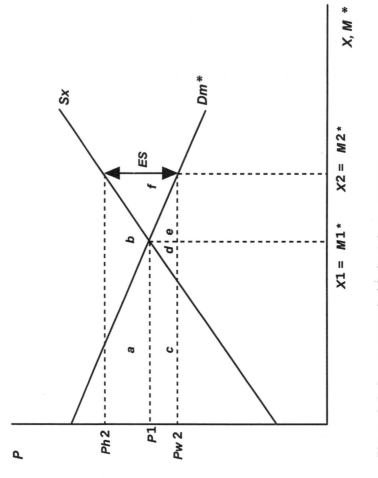

Figure 3.4: An export subsidy by a large country

this clear gain in exporter surplus. However, the European Union faces outlays of $a + \ldots + f$ euros on export subsidies. Consequently, there is an overall decline in welfare equal to $c + \ldots + f$ euros. Area f, as we will see in a moment, represents an efficiency loss that comes about due to induced overtrading. A similar efficiency loss, it will be remembered, arose in the small-country analysis in Section 2.4. Area $c + d + e$ represents an additional terms-of-trade loss to Europe that comes about because the increase in EU exports drives the world price down, which is against the European Union's own interest.

While the overall reduction in EU welfare caused by the export subsidy is important, it is not unduly surprising. It should be emphasized once again that it is vested interests, in this case European grain sector interests rather than the national interest, that drive trade policy. The gain in producer surplus, which exceeds the gain in exporter surplus of $a + b$ euros, provides an immediate benefit to grain farmers and linked firms and provides a long-term benefit to factors, such as land, that are used intensively in grain production.

The central question is not so much why the European Union subsidizes, but why other countries object and/or retaliate. In Figure 3.4, there is an overall welfare gain to non-Europeans or an increase in 'importer surplus' of $c + d + e$ euros arising from the decline in the world price. This is a favourable terms-of-trade effect that is transferred from the European Union; it exactly matches the EU terms-of-trade loss. Non-Europeans gain from the EU export subsidy even though there is a world efficiency loss or loss in world total surplus of f euros.

The overall gain to non-Europeans, however, masks two important considerations. First, the countries that comprise the rest of the world are not homogeneous. Although countries outside the European Union are net importers of grain in aggregate, some individual countries are exporters. Importing countries such as Brazil will definitely experience overall welfare gains, but grain-exporting countries that compete with the European Union, will experience overall welfare losses from the decline in the world price. While the welfare losses in countries that export in competition with the Eurpean Union are significant, they are not the decisive factor in the export subsidy controversy.

The second and more important issue concerns the adverse impact of declining world prices on grain sector interests in all countries outside the European Union, regardless of whether they import or export. The export subsidy can therefore be seen as a policy that 'beggars thy neighbour's farmers'. If the European Union cannot be convinced to cease and desist, grain sector interests in other countries are likely to lobby their own governments for offsetting support measures. In importing countries there will be an impetus to provide protectionist measures, but exporting countries are likely to respond with their own retaliatory export subsidies. This policy perspective is central to an understanding of the grain subsidy wars of the 1980s. Suppose a large country like the United States retaliates against the European Union with an export subsidy of its own. The US export subsidy would raise its home market price and US grain sector interests would gain. The world price, however, would fall further as additional US product entered the international market. This would hurt grain farmers in the European Union and hurt farmers in other countries to an increased degree. The European Union would then be faced with the issue of whether to increase its own export subsidy to protect its farmers. Smaller countries with sizeable export sectors, such as Australia, Canada and Argentina, are likely to find this cross-fire extremely difficult to withstand.

Retaliatory situations such as the grain war described above are known as 'non-cooperative games'. In such non-cooperative games there is strategic interaction between the players. For simplicity, suppose that the European Union and the United States are the only grain producers and exporters. The export subsidy chosen by the United States affects the best choice of export subsidy for the European Union and vise versa. At some point, a Nash equilibrium typically arises where no player regrets its strategy given the strategies pursued by all the other players. In particular, the European Union would not regret its choice of export subsidy given that of the United States and the United States would not regret its choice of export subsidy given that of the European Union in the Nash equilibrium. A general property of such Nash equilibria is that they lead to unexploited gains from mutual cooperation. Notice that in setting its export subsidy, the European Union does not consider the adverse external effect imposed on the United States and the United Stares does not consider the adverse effect on the European Union. Thus limited mutual reductions in export subsidies *must* generate gains for both the European Union and the United States, and the total elimination of all export subsidies *might* generate mutual gains.

This backdrop is vital to understanding the problems of controlling export subsidies. Prior to the Uruguay Round, there were essentially no rules governing export subsidies. In this context our analysis suggests that the European Union, the United States and other agricultural exporters would all gain from initial reductions in export subsidies. Given the differences in circumstances and objectives, however, it is possible that the total elimination of export subsidies was in the interest of the United States and other agricultural exporters, but not the European Union.

In the current negotiations, it certainly appears that the prospect of further reductions in export subsidies by non-EU countries is not sufficiently attractive to prompt the European Union to make further significant concessions on export subsidies. The fact that subsequent rounds of negotiations on reducing export subsidies are likely to be more intractable than the Uruguay Round's over the initial cuts, gives grounds for considerable pessimism. The prospect for further significant cuts to agricultural export subsidies becomes bleaker still so long as the current negotiations remain narrowly focused on agricultural issues, making it more difficult for the European Union to trade off losses on export subsidies for gains elsewhere.

The issue of export subsidies has some important links with the issue of domestic access. Recall that the export subsidy must be augmented with a protectionist measure to prevent or at least limit the inflow of cheaper product from the world market. In the post-Uruguay Round trade environment, these auxiliary measures are limited to tariffs and TRQs. To the extent that the negotiations are successful in improving domestic access for products subject to export subsidies, the outlays on export subsidies would have to increase rather than decrease if the domestic price and, thus, farm-level support is to remain unaffected. Increases in the quantity of product coming in through the 'back door' would necessitate extra product going out through the 'front door'. Consequently, the EU commitment to maintaining export subsidies is likely to increase European Union's intransigence on domestic access.

One possible avenue of escape for the European Union given the mounting pressure to reduce or eliminate export subsidies is to move towards alternative domestic support measures. A problem with this strategy is that many domestic subsidies are also under negotiation. The United States has moved most of its major agricultural support to permissible subsidies. Presumably, the European Union could follow suit. Before turning to the analysis of domestic support measures in Sections 3.7 and 3.8, we first examine some possible indirect modes of export subsidies.

3.5 FOOD SECURITY FOR LESS DEVELOPED COUNTRIES

Both the reductions in export subsidies and the improvements in access that were negotiated in the Uruguay Round were expected and intended to lead to significant increases in world prices for agricultural commodities. Based on the analysis in Section 3.4, it is clear that as exporting countries reduce their export subsidies, supply on the world market falls and the world price rises. Analogously, as importing countries reduce their tariffs and TRQs, demand rises on the world market and, again, the world price rises. However, such increases in world prices have the potential to undermine food security in developing countries that are net food importers, particularly the least developed countries. Further, any diversion of foreign exchange to food imports would necessarily impair development prospects. These problems led to the inclusion of special food security provisions in the URAA. Under fairly general conditions, food aid from developed countries is explicitly permitted. The legitimacy of short-term IMF or World Bank financing of commercial food imports is also affirmed.

Temporary breakdowns in food systems do occur in some developing countries and in such circumstances it is widely acknowledged that food aid has large benefits and few harmful effects for recipient countries. Even in such situations where food aid is fully warranted, however, the effect on the donor country can be broadly similar to an increase in export subsidies. For this reason, we shift the focus to the potential food aid donor country for the moment.

Suppose that the government in a wheat-exporting country, say the European Union, wishes to maintain a home market price, Ph, above the world price, Pw, as shown in Figure 2.4. Such a country faces an excess supply of $Qs1 - Qd1$ tonnes of wheat at the home market price of Ph. As we have seen, the European Union could deal with some or all of the excess supply through an export subsidy equal to the difference between the domestic price and world price, $Ph - Pw$. Alternatively, the EU government could buy up some or all of the excess supply at the home price of Ph. In the latter instance, the EU government could deal with the surplus that it had purchased using any combination of the following five means. First, it could re-sell some or all of the wheat that it had purchased on the world market. Except for differences in transaction costs and transparency, this alternative is, of course, equivalent to an export subsidy. Second, the European Union could store some or all of the surplus wheat. Third, it could give some or all of its wheat away as food aid to foreign countries. Fourth, it could give some or all of the excess wheat away as domestic food aid to domestic residents who would not have purchased wheat at the price of Ph.[2] Finally, the European Union could destroy some or all of its wheat. For simplicity, we focus on the alternatives of export subsidies, storage and foreign food aid in the subsequent discussion.

Suppose that in response to a true emergency situation in a developing country, the European Union decides to give food aid. Further, suppose that it diverts wheat exports (whether subsidized or not) to provide the food aid. In this case, the quantity of wheat supplied on the world market falls by the quantity of food aid. In the limiting situation where all recipients of the food aid would have purchased the exact quantities they receive at the world price, world demand would also fall by the amount given as food aid. Thus, in such an unlikely scenario, the world price would remain unchanged. In the more likely event that some aid recipients would not have been able to buy as much on the world market, world demand will decline by less than world supply and the world price will increase above what it would otherwise have been. In such a situation, wheat sector interests in bystander countries will benefit, and competing export countries will certainly have no cause for complaint.

Now consider what happens if the European Union provides food aid, but continues to export the same quantity of wheat as before whether with subsidies or not. In other words, it reduces the amount that it puts into storage or, if necessary, reduces its inventories of wheat. Consequently, the quantity supplied through regular channels on the world market is unaltered. If none of the foreign recipients of food aid would otherwise have been able to purchase wheat, there will be no impact on either world demand or the world price. As a result, there will be no grounds for complaint by competing wheat exporters such as the United States. In the more likely instance that some of the recipients of food aid would have been able to purchase some wheat in the absence of food aid, world demand will be reduced and the world price will decline. In this case, grain interests in all bystander countries will be adversely affected and competing exporting countries will be especially wary. Nevertheless, in a true food emergency both the world-price effects and the bystander complaints are likely to be minimal.

Finally, consider the effect of the European Union agreeing to reduce subsidized wheat exports by a given amount and then replacing that quantity with food aid. The supply of food moving through regular channels on world markets falls by the agreed amount. On the one hand, the increase in the world price that would have occurred in the absence of food aid will be partially offset because some of the food aid recipients who would have purchased wheat in the absence of aid now purchase less. On the other hand, the world price does rise above the level that would have prevailed in the absence of both the reduction in subsidized exports and the offsetting increase in food aid. Although wheat sector interests in bystander countries do not receive the full increase in the world price that would have been expected in the absence of aid, the difference is likely to be minimal in a true food emergency. Most aid recipients simply would not have been willing or able to make purchases of equal magnitude.

There is, however, a serious danger that the need for food aid could unnecessarily become chronic. Developed countries may have an incentive to provide unnecessary food aid as a substitute for export subsidies to support domestic producer interests. In essence, food aid can act as a safety valve as export subsidies become increasingly constrained. Meanwhile, developing countries may have an incentive to accept unnecessary food aid since the gains to their consumers are likely to be larger than any losses to their producers. In such cases, food aid is likely to cause very close to a one-for-one reduction in world demand and therefore have effects on the world price that are almost equivalent to export subsidies. Of course, the competing sectoral interests in bystander countries will be adversely affected and they will have a very legitimate complaint.

Chronic food aid is likely to have some adverse effects on developing countries even when there is an overall benefit of getting something for nothing. Since producers of products that are direct or close substitutes will find it more difficult to compete, there is a clear adverse effect on rural development in recipient countries. Chronic food aid may also promote dietary deficiencies in developing countries since the products given as food aid are most likely to be those that are in surplus in the developed country rather than what would be imported if consumers could directly express their nutritional preferences. Interestingly, there has been a recent push to expand the Food Aid Convention to include products other than cereals, such as edible oils and dairy products (World Trade Organization, 1999).

There are several reforms to the trading system that could prevent or at least reduce the abuse of food aid without circumscribing legitimate aid. Without minimizing the difficulty of defining *legitimate* aid, simply having a recognized international body identify the aggregate needs of acceptable recipients on a commodity basis would provide helpful transparency. Thereafter, potential donors could be given the option of contributing to the total requirement based on, say, shares of the international market. If some donors declined to contribute, others could increase their subscriptions. If a country wished to provide aid beyond its final authorized contribution, this aid could then be counted as equivalent to an export subsidy. Under current URAA rules, for example, the value of unauthorized aid at world prices should count in the total volume of exports subject to export subsidies that must be reduced by 21 per cent. Similarly, the value of the implicit export subsidy, which is equal to the difference between the donor's domestic price and the world price multiplied by the amount of unauthorized aid, should count in the total outlays on export subsidies that are subject to a 36 per cent reduction. Clearly, these latter measures would offset the current incentives to provide bogus food aid.

On the food security front, the URAA went beyond foreign food aid for developing countries by permitting domestic food aid, public stock-holding of basic foodstuffs, and subsidies for basic foodstuffs that are directed at the rural and/or urban poor. In addition to food security provisions, certain other advantages were provided for developing countries in areas related to food and agriculture (World Trade Organization, 1999). Developed countries committed to an average 43 per cent reduction in tariff and TRQ rates for tropical food products, thus going beyond the average 36 per cent reduction required on food products in general. Meanwhile, developing countries were subject to a 10 per cent minimum cut in tariff rates (rather than the 15 per cent for developed countries) and a 24 per cent average cut in tariff rates (rather than 36 per cent). In addition, developing countries were permitted to set their tariff bindings above the current levels. The least developed countries were not required to make any tariff cuts at all. Developing countries were subject to a minimum 20 per cent reduction in aggregate outlays on export subsidies (rather than 36 per cent for developed countries) and a minimum 14 per cent reduction in the value of goods subject to export subsidies (rather than 21 per cent). While these concessions to developing countries undoubtedly provide a degree of flexibility, the discussion of trade measures in previous chapters suggests that they are often rather dubious 'advantages'. For example, from a domestic policy standpoint developing counties would appear to be ill advised to preserve export subsidies to the extent that is permissible.

For domestic subsidies, the required reduction in the aggregate measure of support (AMS) was set at 13.3 per cent (rather than 20 per cent for developed countries), and the least developed countries were not required to make any cuts in domestic support. In addition, developing countries were given concessions in the calculation of the AMS that effectively excluded some support measures and exempted them from reductions. The *de minimis* level on domestic support that allows a particular commodity to be omitted from the AMS was set at 10 per cent for developing countries rather than 5 per cent. Similarly, rural development initiatives were omitted from the AMS for developing countries. Domestic support is discussed further in Section 3.7, while efforts to control domestic support and reduce the AMS are treated in Section 3.8.

The Trade-Related Intellectual Property (TRIPS) code that formed part of the overall Uruguay Round Agreement provided some flexibility on implementation. Whereas developed countries had one year to comply, developing countries were given five years and the least developed countries 11 years (GATT, 1993, p. 14; Braga, 1995, p. 394). On the other hand, in crucial areas such as world standards for the minimum duration of patents and copyrights, all countries were treated alike. Key concessions that might have made an important difference to developing countries were not forthcoming (Tarvydas et al., 2000). The protection of intellectual property is discussed further in Chapter 4.

3.6 LIMITING THE ACTIONS OF STATE TRADING AGENCIES

Strictly speaking, the topic of state trading agencies or enterprises (STEs) is not unfinished business. State trading agencies are dealt with under Article XVII of the GATT, which is not part of the URAA. This means that the topic is not automatically slated for the continuation of negotiations beginning in 2000. It has been included in this section because the United States feels that it is unfinished business and has made it clear in the strongest terms that it wishes to have it included in any further WTO negotiations on agriculture.

State trading agencies are used extensively by WTO members to manage their agricultural trade. Many developing countries use STEs to manage imports. Some major exporters also use them to conduct their exports. The Canadian Wheat Board and the New Zealand Dairy Board are two examples of longstanding export STEs used by developed countries. The former command economies have large numbers of agricultural STEs, a legacy of the state planning era when prices were set by fiat rather than by markets. As prices were set arbitrarily in command economies, high prices would have encouraged unwanted imports while low prices provided an incentive for state production enterprises to export to obtain higher international prices even when the true resource cost did not warrant exports (Hobbs, Kerr and Gaisford, 1997). Further, due to the fluctuations characteristic of international markets, imports and exports were difficult to incorporate into the material balances approach to planning used by most communist countries (Henderson and Kerr, 1984/85). As a result, command economies made extensive use of STEs. Hence, there is no single model for STEs.

In addition, some STEs are mandated to act as if they are capitalist firms with the goal of maximizing profits, while others operate as adjuncts to foreign policy with no economic rationale underpinning their operations. Most STEs are motivated by a mix of economic and political concerns. After all, countries are only likely to utilize STEs to manage their trade if there is a perceived market failure or some other undesirable outcome produced by market forces.

What is the US complaint against STEs? At the conclusion of the Uruguay Round, US producers were led to believe that they would benefit from large increases in exports. There were two explanations for the predicted rise in US exports. First, US exporters would gain increased access to importers markets as import restrictions were dismantled and domestic levels of support for agriculture reduced. Second, US firms would face less competition in export markets as export subsidies were reduced. Many US exporters now feel they were oversold the likely benefits of the Uruguay Round. From their perspective the promised export opportunities did not materialize. As a result, many are cynical about the WTO process, and explanations for the failure to realize the expected gains are being sought.

One hypothesis put forward by the United States for the failure to gain increased market access is that as formal import barriers have come down, countries have been able to use their importing STEs to continue to deny market access. The United States further hypothesizes that this has been accomplished in two ways. The first is that importing STEs simply add a mark-up in excess of their costs to the price of the products that they purchase in the international market. The effect is the same as a tariff or a variable levy, raising the price to consumers and providing protection for domestic producers. The second method by which the US hypothesizes that STEs restrict inputs is through the imposition of excessive and opaque administrative regimes that must be complied with by those who wish to sell to the STE. In some cases, this red tape can be used as a quantitative constraint that is similar in effect to an import quota; in others it acts to raise the transaction costs for exporters and is similar to a tariff. As a result, the expected gains in market access arising from the Uruguay Round could have been effectively nullified.

The United States has similar concerns that export STEs have been able to nullify the gains in international markets expected to arise from the reduction in export subsidies. Again, it has two hypotheses regarding the benefit-nullifying activities of export STEs. First, STEs may simply be conduits for hidden export subsidies. Second, STEs may have sufficient market power to allow them to capture export markets unfairly. This may be through the use of cross-subsidization – using profits from markets where they can sell above cost to subsidize sales in unprofitable markets. Alternatively, they may be able to sell at a lower than profit-maximizing price to capture a larger share of a market. A profit-maximizing firm will sell a quantity where marginal cost equals marginal revenue whereas a sales-maximizing firm can sell a quantity determined by the point where the average cost cuts the demand curve, a break-even or normal profit yielding price. As private US exporters will profit maximize, they will obtain a smaller market share. In either of the cases cited above, the foreign export STE is able to follow alternative rules, no matter how illogical, because it is an agent of the state.

It should be noted that these are hypotheses regarding STE activity. All four hypotheses are at least plausible explanations of the activities of STEs that could nullify some of the gains expected to arise from the Uruguay Round. It should be noted that the US has offered only hypotheses and not much supporting evidence. Why is this the case?

The existing GATT rules on the activities of STEs are weak. This may not be surprising. When the GATT was established in the late 1940s few member countries had STEs. This was the era before heavy government involvement in economic activity. As a result, little thought was given to them. Over time, governments became much more active in their economies and STEs proliferated. As colonies were freed, their new governments were often very interventionist, with many formally espousing socialism. In agriculture, STEs were seen as a means to break the hold on trade enjoyed by firms associated with the former colonial power, to implicitly tax farmers to pay for industrialization and to isolate domestic markets from the volatility exhibited by international commodity markets. Latterly, some command economies also joined the GATT, bringing with them national trading systems that were the exclusive domain of STEs. The rules for STEs probably needed to be tightened but, as with anything in the GATT, once made, the rules were difficult to change.

In general, GATT principles apply to STEs. They should practice non-discrimination in their buying and selling practices. Their activities should be transparent. In the interpretation of GATT Article XVII, member countries have agreed that they should report the activities of their STEs so that they can be commented upon by member countries. Importing STEs are not allowed to charge a mark-up in excess of the tariff that applies to that category of goods. That is about all; little else is specified. The section on STEs is clearly left over from the old GATT, where problems would be discussed by a 'club of reasonable men' and decided on the basis of economic principles (Kerr and Perdikis, 1995).

The central problem with the existing rules is that they allow the activities of STEs to remain opaque. This lack of transparency annoys the United States because, although it suspects STEs of various nefarious activities, it cannot find out if their suspicions are correct. There are no criteria in Article XVII regarding what activities a country should report.

The result is that what is reported to the WTO is only what countries choose to report. Moreover, the reporting requirement applies only to those agencies that the reporting country considers to be STEs. For example, the European Union does not report the activities of its intervention agencies – and so the United States cannot find out if they are extending elicit export subsidies or not.

Countries are not required to report, for example, the buying price paid by an STE for imports along with its domestic selling price. As a result, it is not possible to determine whether importing STEs are charging a larger mark-up than the bound tariff. The STE might also be using its mark-up ability as a variable levy to protect its market from international market instability – a practice that having bound tariffs is designed to prevent. Countries do not have to report the requirements their STEs impose on exporters or domestic importers. They do not have to report the purchasing strategies of their STEs. As a result, it is not possible to determine if *de facto* import quotas are being imposed.

Countries are not required to explicitly report any non-profit maximizing objectives of their STEs. Hence, it is not possible to determine if they are garnering an 'unfair' share of export markets.

The central question, then, is whether the transparency of the operation of STEs can be improved. The answer is a qualified yes. The WTO could be given the authority to request specific information on the activities of government and quasi-government bodies on its own initiative. It could also make a request if it was asked to do so by a member country. The real question is whether governments would comply with such a request.

There is considerable evidence from experience with regulated industries that they become very adept at seeming to comply without actually complying. There is no reason to believe that the executives of STEs would not become equally adept at hiding information. If countries or the administrators of STEs wished to hide their activities, it is likely that the WTO would expend a great deal of resources to obtain little useful information.

One alternative that has been suggested is that STEs should only be allowed if they operate as commercial (profit-maximizing) enterprises. The question then becomes: Why have them at all? Countries use STEs for the explicit purpose of correcting market failures and pursuing other non-market objectives.

The United States actually understands all the difficulties with regulating STEs. The US proposal, that sells well politically in the US agricultural heartland, is that STEs should not be allowed. Does the US government think that outlawing STEs is feasible? Probably not. It is more likely that its stance on STEs is a bargaining ploy to gain concessions in other areas. It is easy for it to make the demand for abolition because the United States has few STEs. Other trading partners likely have STEs that they don't want closely scrutinized, if for no other reason than that it could prove embarrassing domestically. In the end, countries that make use of STEs may accept some tightening of the rules so that transparency is improved. This may be particularly important given the future accession to the WTO of China and Russia, both of which have a large number of STEs.

3.7 METHODS OF DOMESTIC SUPPORT FOR AGRICULTURE

As an alternative to trade measures such as tariffs and export subsidies, governments can choose from an array of possible domestic support measures for agriculture. However, such domestic support measures typically have a trade impact and as such become a potential matter of negotiation at the WTO. Further, not all domestic support measures are alike. The degree to which and even the direction in which trade is affected by domestic support measures varies enormously. Tables 3.1 and 3.2 show the wide variation in both the domestic support measures used by various countries and the extent of support applied to particular commodities.

Negative levels of domestic support indicate production taxes or broadly equivalent measures.

Table 3.1 Domestic support measures by broad commodity group in 1998 (%)

	European Union	United States	Japan
Wheat	103	101	362
Maize	75	55	--
Other grains	185	88	137
Rice	4	38	8
Oilseeds	95	17	57
Sugar (refined equiv.)	−44	−34	45
Milk	3	19	41
Beef and veal	27	16	4
Pig meat	−4	34	2
Poultry	−3	12	1
Sheep meat	110	4	0
Wool	--	3	--
Eggs	−2	13	2
Other commodities	12	24	5
All commodities	24	24	28

Formula: (Producer NAC/Consumer NAC) −1.
Source: OECD (1999).

We begin our analysis of domestic support measures by examining a simple production subsidy. Figures 3.5 and 3.6 show domestic production subsidies applied in an importing and an exporting sector respectively. Unlike an export subsidy, production destined for domestic consumption as well as export is subsidized. For clarity, we assume that other policy measures are absent so that the consumer and home market prices coincide with the world price, Pw, both before and after the implementation of the production subsidy. While the initial domestic producer price, $Ps0$, is also equal to the world price, the production subsidy of DS dollars per unit raises the producer price above the world and domestic consumer price to $Ps1$ in both Figure 3.5 and Figure 3.6.

The increase in the producer price occasions a short-run supply response from $Qs0$ to $Qs1$ and a larger supply response to $Qs2$ in the long run.

Economics for Trade Negotiations

Table 3.2 Producer support measures by policy type in 1998 (US$billion)

	European Union	United States	Japan
Trade-related support measures			
1. All market-price support (net payments of consumers plus government)	80.4 (62)	23.5 (50)	44.8 (91)
Domestic support measures			
2. Payments based on output	4.2 (3)	2.7 (6)	1.2 (2)
3. Payments based on area planted/animal numbers	29.8 (23)	2.9 (6)	0.0 (0)
4. Payments based on overall farming income	0.0 (0)	1.1 (2)	0.0 (0)
Subtotal: Production-related domestic support (Rows 2–4)	34.0 (26)	6.7 (14)	1.2 (2)
5. Payments based on input use	9.9 (8)	4.7 (10)	2.2 (4)
6. Payments based on input constraints	4.1 (3)	2.0 (4)	0.9 (2)
7. Payments based on historical entitlements	0.8 (1)	8.5 (18)	0.0 (0)
8. Miscellaneous	0.7 (1)	1.5 (3)	0.0 (0)
Subtotal: Domestic support (Rows 2–8)	49.5 (38)	23.4 (50)	4.3 (9)
Total: Trade-related & domestic support (Rows 1–8)	129.8 (100)	47.0 (100)	49.1 (100)
Proportion: Low-trade distortion support (Rows 6–7)/(Rows 2–8)	(10)	(45)	(21)

Note: Figures in brackets indicate percentages.
Source: OECD (1999).

Consumption remains unchanged at Qd because the consumer price does not change. In Figure 3.5, imports, which are initially $Qd - Qs0$, fall to $Qd - Qs1$ in the short run and fall further to $Qd - Qs2$ in the long run. If the supply response was large enough, a country that initially imported could switch to exporting after the production subsidy was imposed. In Figure 3.6, exports, which are initially $Qs0 - Qd$, rise to $Qs1 - Qd$ in the short run and rise further to $Qs2 - Qd$ in the long run.

While the production subsidies clearly distort trade, their impact is smaller than corresponding trade measures because only production and not consumption is affected. Compare the tariff shown in Figure 2.7 with the

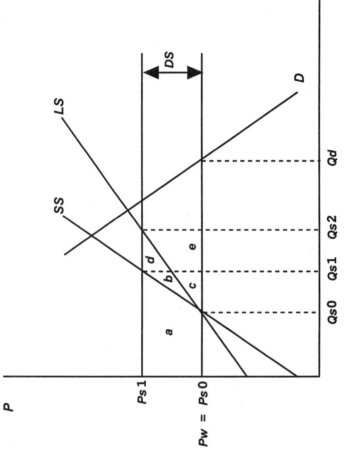

Figure 3.5: A production subsidy in an import-competing sector

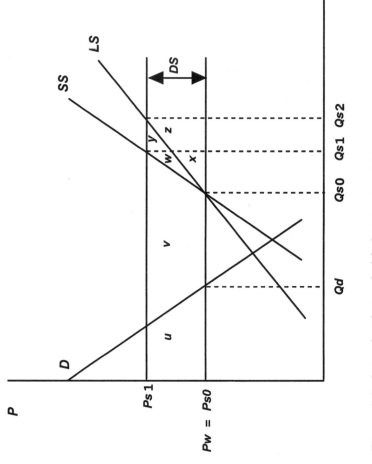

Figure 3.6: A production subsidy in an export sector

production subsidy in Figure 3.5. If the two measures are of the same size the increase in production will be the same, but the tariff will reduce imports more because consumption declines. Similarly, the export subsidy shown in Figure 2.8 can be compared with the production subsidy in Figure 3.6. Once again, the increase in production will be the same if the two measures are of the same size, but the export subsidy will increase exports more because consumption declines.

When the production subsidy is applied to an importing sector as shown in Figure 3.5, producer surplus rises by a dollars but government outlays on production subsidies are equal to $a + b + c$ dollars in the short run. Consumers are unaffected, since they do not experience a change in price. In spite of the short-run producer benefit, which is a powerful motive for the policy, there is an overall loss to the subsidizing country of $b + c$ dollars. In the long run, rents accruing to inputs used intensively in the subsidized sector rise by $a + b + d$ dollars, but government expenditures on subsidies are $a + ... + e$ dollars making for a larger efficiency loss of $c + e$ dollars. A fully equivalent analysis of the producer, budgetary and overall effects of production subsidies applied to an exporting sector could be conducted using Figure 3.6. The short-run subsidy outlays of $u + ... + x$ dollars exceeds the gain in producer surplus of $u + v$ dollars leading to an overall welfare loss of $w + x$ dollars. Similarly, the long-run subsidy outlays of $u + ... + z$ dollars exceeds the gain in rents of $u + v + w + y$ dollars and implies efficiency loss of $x + z$ dollars.

In Chapter 2, we saw that domestic market-price supports or floor prices applicable to producers and consumers alike were broadly equivalent to tariffs or export subsidies. We can now use Figures 3.5 and 3.6 to show that domestic producer-price support policies are broadly equivalent to production subsidies. The key difference between a producer-price support and a market-price support is that the producer-price support is only applicable to producers and not consumers. As a result, any divergence between the administered producer price set by the government and the market price necessitates deficiency payments by the government. These deficiency payments are analogous to production subsidy payments. Suppose that the producer support price is set at $Ps1$. In Figure 3.5, the deficiency payments will be equal to $a + b + c$ dollars in the short run and $a + ... + e$ dollars in the long run. Similarly, in Figure 3.6, deficiency payments are equal to $u + ... + x$ in the short run and $u + ... + z$ in the long run. Thus, the producer-price support policy is fully equivalent to a production subsidy if demand, supply and the world price are not subject to variability. When demand, supply and/or the world price are variable, the producer price remains constant with the former but not with the latter policy. In effect, a production subsidy of variable magnitude is required as an auxiliary to a domestic producer-price support policy, just as a tariff and potentially an export subsidy of variable magnitude was required as an auxiliary to a domestic market-price support.

There are numerous other domestic subsidies that enhance production and distort trade in a manner that is similar to production subsidies. Some examples include subsidies on the utilization of inputs such as fertilizer and subsidies on land or soil improvements. While the supply price would remain unaltered (for example, at $Ps0 = Pw$ in Figures 3.5 and 3.6) with such input subsidies, the supply curve would shift to the right. Once again output would rise, leading to a decline in imports, a switch to exports or an increase in exports. Consequently, subsidies on input use or input improvement, like production subsidies, will be of legitimate concern to trade partners. This does not mean, however, that all domestic support measures are production enhancing and thereby import reducing or export increasing.

The trade-distorting effects and inefficiencies associated with production subsidies themselves could be reduced or possibly even eliminated by making subsidy payments subject to quantity limits. For example, headage payments could be based on a fixed maximum number of animals and acreage payments on a fixed maximum area planted. In either Figure 3.5 or 3.6, if subsidies were only paid on $Qs0$ units of output or less, production would not rise at all and trade flows would be unaffected. However, the difficulties and costs of administering such limits stand to be non-trivial whether the overall subsidy limit is applied on a first-come, first-served basis or eligibility for subsidies is allocated at the farm level. A further complication with headage and acreage payments is that output is not directly constrained. For example, both animal size and the intensity of land use can be varied.

Another possibility is to have subsidy payments based on historic, rather than current, levels of production. The United States has increased its use of such subsidies, and some of the European Union's compensatory payments also fit into this category (see Table 3.2). Such subsidies are 'de-coupled' from current production to the extent that they do not affect output in the short run. Subsidies based on historic output levels, however, are unlikely to be fully de-coupled from output in the long run (Kerr, 1988). These subsidies are generally non-transferable and tied to continued activity in agriculture. Further, like all subsidies, they are typically imposed in a setting where there would otherwise be an incentive for firms to exit the industry. Since the subsidies based on historic production levels are typically designed to keep some firms in business that would otherwise go bankrupt, they do increase long-run output above the level that otherwise would have prevailed. Consequently, imports will be lower or exports will be higher than would otherwise have been expected.[3]

Domestic support measures can also be designed to reduce rather than increase output. Subsidies such as land set-asides are effectively payments to reduce input use. A land set-aside would not introduce a wedge between the supply price and the domestic market price for the product, but it would reduce output by shifting the supply curve to the left. In this case there would be a reduction in exports, a switch to imports or an increase in imports. Since the world price would tend to be pushed upward rather than downward, the impact on foreign producers would be favourable and trade partners would have no grounds for complaint based on producer interests.

On products that are readily tradable, production quotas or other restraints on output can potentially be used to limit or curtail even the production and trade responses to domestic support measures such as production subsidies. Similarly, production quotas can be used in conjunction with trade measures such as tariffs and export subsidies to limit or curtail the production response. In the case where production quotas are combined with trade measures, however, trade flows will be affected even if production is not. Recall that trade measures result in a reduction in consumption as well as an increase in output. When a tariff raises the domestic market price, production quotas could hold domestic output constant, but imports would still fall due to the decline in consumption. Similarly, when an export subsidy raises the domestic market price, exports will rise due to the decrease in consumption even if production quotas hold domestic output constant. Nonetheless production restraints may at least limit the trade-distorting effects of other policies.

On products that are not readily tradable, such as fresh milk, production quotas could potentially be used as a domestic support measure in isolation from other policies. Since milk is perishable, transport and handling costs are likely to increase as the volume of imports rises. While the residual demand facing the domestic dairy industry net of imports will be more elastic than the domestic demand curve, it will not be perfectly elastic. As the domestic market price rises, more imports enter the market but some demand remains to be filled by domestic producers. Thus, if production quotas are imposed so as to reduce the domestic output below the free-market equilibrium level, the domestic market price will rise. The loss in consumer surplus will outweigh the gain in quota rents, causing a loss in overall welfare that is similar to a monopoly. While the short-run producer gains may drive policy formulation, the quota rents will be capitalized into the value of the quotas in the long run, as discussed in Chapter 2. The original quota holders would benefit, but new entrants and producers *per se* would be no better off due to the imputed or actual costs of the milk quota.

The production quotas on milk are not trade-neutral. In the absence of any accompanying restrictions on trade, imports will rise in response to the higher domestic price. This latter effect will remain minimal provided that the difficulties in transport and distribution remain great. Even so, the production quotas on their own are import enhancing. Alternatively, the production quota, in isolation, would be export reducing if the country was initially on an export basis.[4] Of course, the central problem with production quotas in general and milk quotas in particular is that transport and distribution costs, while still significant, have fallen considerably. As the residual demand facing the domestic industry becomes increasingly elastic, countries have typically faced the alternatives of allowing a decline in producer support or imposing auxiliary trade measures to forestall an increase in imports.

The economic analysis of domestic support is complicated further by the so-called 'multi-functionality' of agriculture. Norway, the Nordic members of the European Union and Japan in particular have alleged that in addition to regular private goods that go through market channels, agriculture produces environmental, cultural and amenity benefits which are public goods that would be underprovided in the absence of government support. For example, it is claimed that small-scale Japanese farms generate flood control benefits, and it is said that the hedgerows and stone walls of traditional UK farms provide a scenic landscape amenity that benefits the general population (Morris and Anderson, 1999). While the basic multi-functionality argument is economically plausible, there are two key issues. First, the magnitude of the multi-functional benefits is at issue. If these benefits are small in reality, the entire argument may be an elaborate ploy by governments in the Nordic countries and Japan to preserve domestic subsidies and protect their agricultural producers in the WTO negotiations. Certainly, countries outside of Europe and Japan have been suspicious.

The second, more fundamental issue, is that subsidies that directly target agricultural output would at best be an imperfect or second-best solution to the market failure associated with multi-functionality. Since the problem is the underprovision of multi-functional public benefits rather than the underproduction of agricultural outputs *per se*, the activities leading to multi-functional benefits should be subsidized directly. Since the crux of the argument is that specific farm-level activities create multifunctional social benefits that exceed the private benefits realized by farmers in producing agricultural outputs, it is these specific activities rather than production in general that merit subsidies. Further, the magnitude of the subsidy on any particular activity should just compensate farmers for the difference between the marginal social and private benefits.

That is to say, subsidies should be directed to flood control activities or hedgerow maintenance. If farm output is subsidized instead, the improvement in multi-functional benefits will be smaller and there may even be a reduction in benefits. To take an extreme but conceivable example, if production subsidies led to the consolidation of farms, flood control benefits might be eroded or hedgerows might disappear. While the multi-functionality argument does legitimately complicate the broad issue of domestic support, it does not legitimize direct production subsidies.

It is safe to conclude that domestic support measures almost inevitably affect trade flows and therefore are a legitimate topic for trade negotiations. Different domestic support measures not only differ in the magnitude and timing of their trade effects but also in the direction of those effects. Further, some domestic subsidies may correct market failures rather than impairing efficiency. Consequently, there is no simple all-encompassing answer to the problem of domestic support at the WTO. We now turn to the complex issue of controlling levels of domestic support at the WTO.

3.8 CONTROLLING LEVELS OF DOMESTIC SUPPORT: THE CASE OF MULTICOLOURED BOXES

The limits put on the ability of governments to subsidize farmers will be one of the most hotly contested issues for the negotiations that commenced in 2000. The ability to provide subsidies is a major role of governments. It is a sovereign right that governments protect closely. They will resent and resist international limits on their actions with regard to subsidization. It is clear, however, that subsidies can distort international trade just as easily as border measures. Just as 'beggar thy neighbour' tariff wars can inhibit economic prosperity and lead to a heightening of international political tensions, so too can 'beggar thy neighbour' subsidy wars. Hence, it makes no sense to have international controls on border measures without addressing the question of trade-distorting subsidies. The GATT, and subsequently the WTO, thus has a role in designing rules for the use of trade-distorting subsidies. A distinction is made in this chapter between export subsidies and domestic measures of support. This is because the WTO effectively bans export subsidies and their import counterpart of subsidies whose receipt is contingent on the use of domestic rather than foreign inputs.

Domestic support policies have no direct trade-distorting intent and hence in theory are allowed by the WTO. This reflects governments' basic right to provide subsidies. The WTO should only get involved if the subsidy distorts trade. The problem, as outlined in the previous section, is that any subsidy applied to a tradable good is likely to be trade distorting over the long run. This is because even subsidies that are not directly tied to production, such as lump sum payments based on historic use of the land base or the number of head of livestock, at some specific point in time keep more resources in an industry than would be the case without the subsidy being paid. They keep firms in business that would otherwise exit the industry, thereby increasing supply in competition with imports from other countries or adding to exports. It is not possible to determine the exact extent of this distortion over the long run due to the possibility of the entrance of new producers once the value of fixed assets such as farmland has depreciated. These new entrants could replace some or possibly all of the production of those firms that have exited.

Although considerable effort was put into attempts to define theoretically de-coupled subsidies, this proved to be an intellectual dead end when the long run was considered (Kerr, 1988). Short-run de-coupled subsidies can be identified, however, and they provide a loose theoretical basis for the current argument over the types of subsidies that should be allowed.

Given that non-trade-distorting subsidies could not be identified, at the Uruguay Round the member countries of the GATT abandoned the formal attempt to provide a coherent economic argument regarding what types of subsidies would be condoned. Instead, they decided to arbitrarily assign different subsidy delivery mechanisms to various categories. As suggested above, export subsidies were put in the Prohibited category (sometimes known by its traffic light shorthand of 'red box' or 'GATT red'). Of course, a transition phase was allowed, so the red box is still officially empty for agriculture.

According to what was agreed at the Uruguay Round, Non-Actionable ('green box', or 'GATT green') subsidies are allowed without limit and are not subject to complaint by trade partners. Actionable ('amber – sometimes 'yellow' – box or 'GATT yellow') subsidies are potentially subject to complaint if they exceed 5 per cent (*de minimis*) of the value of the good. If the complainant is an importing country, its normal recourse would be to apply a countervailing duty against the subsidized imports. (Countervailing duties are discussed further in Chapter 4.) However, if the country exports a non-agricultural good on a competing basis, it can lodge a complaint related to actionable domestic subsidies with the WTO.

It was agreed that in principle agriculture would ultimately come under the general WTO disciplines, including the rules on subsidies. The URAA, however, as discussed above, allows for a transition to the general rules of trade for agricultural subsidies. For domestic subsidies, the transition for agriculture was made more complex, for three closely related reasons. First, the cuts to export subsidies had the potential to inadvertently reward those countries that happened to rely more heavily on trade-distorting domestic subsidies. Second, in reducing export subsidies, there was a potential danger that countries would simply switch to domestic subsidies. Third, there was the potential danger of WTO dispute settlement processes being swamped by large numbers of complaints from competing agricultural exporters. To address these issues, it was decided that actionable domestic subsidies on agricultural goods, unlike those on non-agricultural goods, would be subject to explicit monitoring and cuts. As a *quid pro quo*, countries that export on a competing basis are not to seek redress for actionable domestic subsidies to agriculture at the WTO.

The green box includes subsidies that are non-industry or commodity specific, such as education and research as well as subsidies that have public good aspects, such as those provided for disease control, food safety and food security. Subsidies that provide assistance to disadvantaged areas are also in this category. A special provision is made in the case of agriculture for direct payments to producers.

Subsidies not categorized in the *red* or *green* boxes are considered Actionable. The first step in the transition to general WTO disciplines for Actionable subsidies was a 20 per cent reduction. This meant that at the start of negotiations in 2000 more than 80 per cent of the value of pre-Uruguay Round Actionable subsidies remained in developed countries. On an individual commodity basis, many of these far exceeded the 5 per cent *de minimis* levels allowed in the general WTO rules. Although a 20 per cent reduction in domestic levels of support was agreed at the Uruguay Round, a further list of 'blue box' subsidies was exempted from the calculation of the 20 per cent slated for reduction. These were agricultural subsidies that were not to be counted in the aggregate measure of support (AMS) used to determine the base value for the reduction in domestic subsidies. As a result, more than 80 per cent remain eligible for the next phase of transition. An even greater proportion is available in developing countries. As no restraints were put on least developed countries, 95 per cent of their domestic subsidies are available for negotiation.

The remaining difference between the levels of subsidy reduction agreed in the URAA and the general WTO rules on domestic subsidies sets the limits within which negotiations will take place. Countries wishing to improve international access for their products will push to have the range of subsidies in the green box reduced and, if that is not achievable, will be insistent that they are not expanded. They will want the blue box closed. Again, if that cannot be achieved, then they will want the range of subsidies placed in the box reduced and certainly will not want them expanded. While these countries would like to move immediately to the *de minimis* level on a product-by-product basis for Actionable subsidies, as a fall-back position they will want a specific timetable for the transition to *de minimis* levels. They will not want to continue with the existing transition mechanism of aggregate subsidy reduction commitments, because it allows countries to offset small subsidy reductions for particularly sensitive products with larger commitments for less sensitive products. If aggregate subsidy reduction commitments cannot be achieved, these countries will want a strict timetable for staged elimination and will not want another interim stage that will then have to be subject to a further round of negotiations.

On the other hand, countries that wish to continue to support their farmers at high levels and, implicitly to deny access to their markets will want to stop the transition process or at least have it require minimum changes to their subsidy programmes. The easiest way for them to avoid having to reduce their subsidies would be to have the green box opened up to include a greater range of subsidies. This would allow them to avoid reductions in their subsidies and even allow the flexibility to increase them. They can be expected to push hard for this option. They will also push for the retention and, if possible, expansion of the blue box. This would allow them to circumvent any commitments they must make to reduce their aggregate levels of support further by altering subsidy programmes to fit into the blue box exemptions.

Countries that do not wish to reduce subsidies will also wish to keep as much flexibility as possible in apportioning subsidy cuts among products. This will allow them to continue to fully protect politically sensitive products. They will also want to go slow on the rate of reductions in subsidies and to avoid any fixed timetables for transition. They will only want to move to a new, lower stage, with further reductions taking place after an additional set of negotiations. They will also wish to avoid any firm commitments to further negotiations on reducing agricultural subsidies.

Hence, the battle lines are clearly drawn and there does not appear to be much common ground. The most important issue will be what types of subsidies will be allowed in the green box. Whatever is placed on the list of non-actionable subsidies is likely to remain there permanently. Everything else that is agreed to will simply be a stage in the transition process and will be open to future negotiation – even if no timetable for negotiation is agreed.

The questions surrounding domestic levels of support are clearly yesterday's issues. All of the difficult intellectual work on subsidies was done in the lead-up to and during the Uruguay Round. This does not mean that the negotiations will not be difficult. They are likely to be some of the most acrimonious at the new negotiations. The negotiations themselves, however, will simply be old-fashioned horse-trading. There are no inventive solutions available or mutually beneficial directions in which to move. Within agriculture, it is give and take and not *quid pro quo*. Those who want better market access have little to offer those who wish to continue to subsidize their farmers to a high degree. What they have to offer will have to come from outside agriculture.

The negotiations on domestic levels of support should, however, be considered within the broad context of the WTO. The current situation in agriculture is very similar to that which existed for tariffs when the GATT was originally negotiated. Tariffs were very high and had not been subject to any international discipline. The waivers granted to agriculture mean that negotiations are at their earliest stage. The transition to lower subsidies began only six years ago. It took GATT members almost 50 years to dismantle the very high levels of tariffs put in place in the interwar period or even prior to it. While the slow rate of progress on tariff reduction was frustrating for those who could see their commercial opportunities being limited by tariffs, over the long run progress continued – and still continues – to be made. The conclusion of every round of negotiations has been perceived as limited in achievement and has led to worries that it may be the last. Taken together, however, the rounds were a considerable success. The trick for both sides is to ensure that progress continues to be made on the transition of agricultural subsidies towards general WTO norms.

3.9 DOES CAPITALIZATION INFLUENCE THE NEGOTIATIONS?

In many countries, agricultural sectors have been supported by a vast assortment of trade policy and domestic support measures. The effect of trade policy is to raise the home market price above the world price, while the effect of domestic support is to raise producer prices above the home market price and/or reduce production costs relative to the home market price. The analysis in Chapter 2 demonstrated that the benefits of higher prices tend to become capitalized into the value of assets that are used intensively or exclusively in agriculture, such as land. The capitalization of the benefits of past agricultural policy initiatives will have a profound effect on current WTO negotiations on agriculture.

When the government intervenes in the market to mitigate the effects of poor international competitiveness, it will provide a benefit to individual firms. As firms are unlikely to have exactly the same cost structure, the benefits conferred by the policy intervention will not be the same for all firms. More efficient firms will receive the greatest benefit. While it is possible that the level of support provided by the trade policy intervention will only be sufficient to return the most efficient firms to a position of profitability, this would leave all less efficient firms still making losses. As it is the less efficient firms that suffer the greatest losses from international competition, they tend to lobby governments most ardently for relief. Hence, support tends to be set at levels that allow many, although possibly not all, less efficient farms to remain solvent.

Farmers' costs can be viewed as a continuum ranging from the least efficient to the most efficient. These differences in costs may be attributable to location, climate, soil fertility, previously acquired machinery, entrepreneurial ability, technological adaptability and so on. The level of support is typically set sufficiently high to sustain a considerable proportion of less efficient farmers. Farmers who are more efficient than those for whom the level of support simply provides a normal rate of return will earn in excess of a normal rate of return in the short run. In the long run, the policy benefits that accrue to efficient farms will tend to be capitalized into the value of relatively fixed assets such as land as discussed in Chapter 2.

The effects of government policy interventions can be illustrated using Figure 3.7, which shows two representative firms. Firm (a) is said to be efficient while firm (b) is inefficient. The pre-intervention long-run average cost curve for firm (a), $LACa°$, is lower than that of firm (b), $LACb$. At the world price, Pw, firm (a) is just competitive, but firm (b) would not be able to cover its costs and would have to exit from the industry unless the government intervene in the market. Suppose that as a result of lobbying, the government imposed a trade-related or domestic support measure that raised the price obtained by producers to *Ps*. At this price, farm (b) would earn a normal profit and would be able to remain in the industry in the long run.[5] If the government is committed to maintaining the viability of farms with cost structures similar to that of farm (b), it must keep the domestic price at or above *Ps*.

Farm (a) can, of course, also sell its output at *Ps* once the support measure is in place. Consequently, farm (a) earns supernormal profit in the short run. However, the existence of this benefit has considerable long-run ramifications. Super-normal profits provide a signal that more resources should be committed to the farming activity that firm (a) is engaged in. New farmers will wish to enter the industry if they are capable of producing at any average cost less than *Ps*. As firms scramble to enter, they will over time bid up of the price of relatively fixed inputs such as land. Individuals who are not in the industry and who could be equal in efficiency to the existing efficient firm need to acquire land to enter the industry and reap the super normal profits, which are the benefit provided by the support policy. New entrants will begin to bid against each other to rent or buy land. The payment to rent or buy land is a real cost for new entrants, and increases their average cost above *LACa°*. New entrants will continue to bid up rents until the cost rises to the point where there is no super normal profit left. In Figure 3.7 this is illustrated by an increase in average cost to *LACa'*. In the long run, the support measure leads to additional actual or imputed rents on land of shaded area *Ra'*, which amounts to *Ps* − *Pw* on each unit of output sold.

The additional rents attributable to the policy measures accrue annually over the duration of the support policy. The net present value of a future stream of annual benefits that accrue at the year end can be calculated using the formula:

$$NPV = \sum_{t=1}^{T} \frac{B}{(1+r)^t}$$

where *B* represents the annual net benefit, *r* denotes the annual interest rate, *t* denotes the year and *T* is the number of years over which benefits are

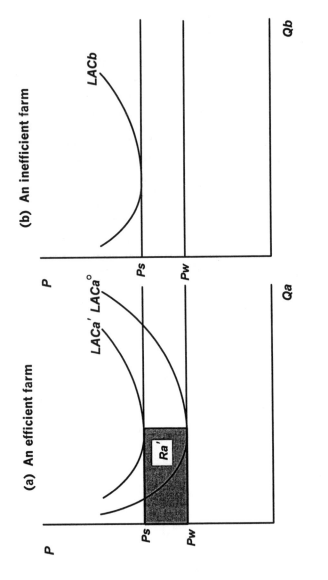

FIGURE 3.7: Capitalization re-visited

received. Suppose that farm (a)'s land will generate an extra 100 000 francs in rent per year. If the interest rate is 8 per cent and the policy will be in place for five years, the net present value of the policy-derived rents is:

$$NPV = \frac{100000}{(1+0.08)^1} + \frac{100000}{(1+0.08)^2} + \frac{100000}{(1+0.08)^3} + \frac{100000}{(1+0.08)^4} + \frac{100000}{(1+0.08)^5}$$
$$= 399268.$$

Under these circumstances, a prospective land buyer would be willing to pay almost 400 000 francs more than in the absence of support measures. As we saw in Chapter 2, this additional 400 000 francs represents the capitalization of the policy benefits into the value of the land.

If world prices were expected to rise and/or production costs were expected to decline sufficiently over the five-year duration, support policies could indeed be withdrawn without undermining the long-term viability of farm (b). If prices were temporarily depressed on world markets, it follows that a temporary policy measure would be adequate. In agriculture, however, the cumulative effects of significant technological improvement, technological diffusion to developing countries and low price elasticities of demand tend to make for long-term declines in real prices. Thus the problems facing inefficient farms are likely to become more, rather than less, pronounced. In the event of further reductions in world prices or increases in input costs, governments are likely to encounter pressure to increase rather than reduce levels of support.

Suppose that the support policy will continue indefinitely rather than being terminated after five years. When the policy rents are permanent, the extent of capitalization on farm (a) is greater. The present value of a perpetual stream of rents equal to 100 000 francs per year at 8 per cent interest is:

$$NPV = \frac{B}{r} = \frac{100000}{0.08} = 1250000.$$

The piece of land would be worth an additional 1.25 million francs because of the support policy. As time passes, more new entrants will come in and more existing farms will turn over due to retirements. Since more and more of the efficient farms will have the cost structure shown by *LACa'* in Figure 3.7, the removal of the support policy will lead to losses for these type (a) farms as well. Whereas initially only the inefficient farms faced bankruptcy, now many of the efficient farms are threatened as well. Thus the support policy develops considerable inertia over time.

If the support policy were removed, land values would eventually return to their original levels. Thus surviving farms of the efficient type and subsequent entrants who buy the now cheaper land would again be viable in the long run. However, this does not lessen the short-term disruption that would face efficient producers or reduce the real resource costs that would be associated with bankruptcy. It would also be of little consolation to existing efficient farmers who are likely to face financial ruin.

In the event of insolvency, farmers – whether efficient or inefficient – typically face devastating capital losses as well as the loss of current income. Effort is extremely important in agriculture yet very costly to monitor. Consequently, it is prohibitively expensive for the owner of the land or other agricultural assets (that is, the principal) to write rental contracts that are contingent on the optimum effort of the farmer (that is, the agent). One result of this principal-agent problem is that farmers tend to be owners of farm assets as well as being farm operators. There is far less separation between ownership and control or management in agriculture than in most other sectors of the economy. Consequently, farmers tend to be underdiversified in the sense that a very high proportion of their wealth is held in farm assets, such as land, structures and machinery. In addition, the farmer's home is typically located on the farm. In times of depressed farming, the demand for this asset is also likely to fall. As a result when farms fail the farmers often lose everything, not just their livelihoods. This often provides a politically compelling rationale for governments to implement support policies.

Prior to the Uruguay Round, agriculture operated under GATT waivers and countries were allowed to provide farmers with policy benefits in the form of protection from imports, export subsidies and trade-distorting domestic subsidies. The value of those benefits was capitalized into the value of farmland. As we have seen, the URAA made modest progress in limiting trade-distorting policy measures, but high levels of support remain. Table 3.2 shows that the total annual support provided to agriculture in the European Union in 1998 was US$129.8 billion, in the United States it was US$47.0 billion and in Japan U$49.1 billion. The annual support will typically exceed the extra policy-induced annual rents, but they are likely to be of the same order of magnitude. We can make simple back-of-the-envelope estimates of capitalization by assuming that rents are 75 per cent of the policy-induced receipts of producers and discounting at the fairly high real rate of interest of 8 per cent to allow for the fact that there is a risk that the support measures will be removed. This would put policy-induced capitalization at US$1.217 trillion for the European Union, US$0.441 trillion for the United States and US$0.461 trillion for Japan.

The policy-inflated value of farmland becomes part of farmers' assets, but the real question is who benefits from the support measures over the long run. The major beneficiaries are those who owned farmland at the time the policies were put in place and who subsequently sold their farmland. New entrants paid for those trade policy benefits when they purchased their land and do not receive ongoing benefits from the existence of the policy.

The capitalization of trade policy benefits makes it difficult to abandon support policies in the current WTO negotiations. These are real costs that must be met by those who purchased high-priced farmland. Many will have borrowed to pay for the land and the mortgage payments are an ongoing expense. Abandoning the trade policy will mean a depreciation in the value of farmland and threaten the financial viability of recent entrants.

In addition, financial institutions will have lent against the value of farmland. Removal of the trade policy could lead to widespread defaults on loans and threaten financial institutions with a high proportion of agricultural loans in their portfolio. Japan is particularly sensitive to this problem given the long duration and high levels of protection provided by its agricultural policies and its recent experience with financial institutions that had lent against overvalued urban real estate. In Japan and the European Union, there has been policy-induced overinvestment in the agricultural input and processing sectors. Further, in the European Union there has been a dramatic overinvestment in storage facilities as surplus product has been purchased by intervention agencies. Any reductions in support arising from the WTO negotiations threaten these investments as well.

While capitalization may never explicitly make the headlines, it will dramatically affect the underlying substance of the negotiations. Put simply, it is politically impossible to abandon farmers and firms in linked sectors. The European Union in particular seems already to have adopted an intransigent position. Any concessions it makes are likely to come in the form of gradual reductions in support and/or compensation for the removal of support. The post-Uruguay Round movement by the European Union to direct payments to farmers with similar or even higher levels of budgetary expenditures can be interpreted as an attempt to defend farmers' asset base.

Economics for Trade Negotiations
3.10 THE NEGOTIATING POSITIONS OF THE MAJOR PLAYERS

3.10.1 The Players

The major economic powers will shape both the agenda for the negotiations and their progress to a greater degree than other countries. They all have strong positions on agriculture. Even with declining farm populations, agricultural issues still command considerable attention in their domestic politics, far more attention than the farm populations would seem to justify. Unlike many developing countries, none have large proportions of their economic activity generated by agriculture. Agricultural trade is not crucial for the economies of any of them.

In all of the major economic powers, however, trade policy is seen as an adjunct to domestic agricultural policy and agricultural trade is expected to contribute to the goals of domestic agricultural policy. The overwhelming thrust of domestic agricultural policy is common – to slow the process of shedding labour; that is farmers, from the agricultural sector. The exit of farm populations has been an ongoing phenomenon for over a century and is the result of sustained technological change in agriculture. As with any change, it creates social disruption and both winners and losers. Agricultural policy, however well or badly designed, has had the objective of reducing social disruption and mitigating the costs for losers from the process of technological change. Agricultural trade policy has taken as it credo that imports are 'bad' because they mean fewer farmers and that exports are 'good' because they mean more farmers. Broad-based welfare concerns have held little sway in the making of agricultural trade policy. The negotiating positions of the major players at the WTO reflect their domestic policy concerns.

Japan and the European Union are protectionist in their outlook on agricultural trade. While the United States has some protectionist programmes in its agricultural trade policy, it is generally pro-liberalization because it is a net exporter. Japan is a large importer. The European Union would be a large net importer if it were not for the heavy degree of support provided to farmers by the CAP. These very different situations make it difficult for the major economic powers to find common ground.

While not a major economic power, the Cairns Group of mid-sized agricultural exporting countries have come to represent a significant voice at the negotiations. As a result, their concerns are worth examining. A number of central and eastern European countries will have a particularly difficult time developing a strategy for their negotiations given the uncertainties surrounding their accession to the European Union.

3.10.2 The European Union

The European Union's agricultural trade policy is entirely subsumed by its domestic agricultural policy – the CAP – and is an adjunct to it. The CAP provides a wide spectrum of agricultural products with prices that are above those that would prevail in world markets. Farmers in the European Union are also provided with more price stability than is exhibited by many international markets for agricultural commodities. To sustain high and stable prices, import measures must be used. Price stability tends to require quantitative restrictions or variable levies on imports rather than unchanging, WTO sanctioned bound tariffs. It was agreed at the Uruguay Round that all quantitative restrictions and variable levies would be converted to tariffs. As an interim measure, greater access was negotiated under TRQs. These are still required to support the CAP and the European Union can be expected to negotiate vigorously for their retention and to keep TRQ levels small.

Under general WTO rules, export subsidies are prohibited. However, the CAP's high price regime is sufficient to encourage (often large) production surpluses over a wide range of products. One of the means used to manage these surpluses is for the European Union to export them under subsidy. These subsidized exports compete in third markets with US products and products of members of the Cairns Group. Hence, they have been a major issue of contention at the negotiations. As a compromise, export subsidies were reduced somewhat in the Uruguay Round negotiations but are still allowed at an expenditure value of at least 60 per cent of their pre-Uruguay Round levels. As CAP reforms have not brought about a consistent equilibrium between supply and demand, and the surpluses continue for many products, the European Union can be expected to resist further reductions in export subsidy levels (Swinbank, 1999).

Domestic levels of agricultural support will also be subject to negotiation. The continuation of the blue box compromise, which allows policies involving direct payments to farmers to be exempted from domestic support reduction calculations, will be hotly contested. The European Union needs to keep these exemptions while the United States feels it has converted its blue box subsidies to those which fall into the green box of allowable subsidies under the WTO rules.

The European Union is also currently dealing with the difficult problem of consumers' and environmentalist' acceptance of biotechnology. It has asked if the WTO's Agreement on the Application of Sanitary and Phyto-Sanitary Measures can be re-opened to deal with this issue (Perdikis, Kerr and Hobbs, 1999). The United States has rejected this request out of hand. Given that a number of countries are having to deal with the biotechnology issue, it may well be forced on to the agenda. This issue is dealt with in greater detail in Chapter 4.

3.10.3 The United States

The agricultural community in the United States is suspicious and cynical about the next round of agricultural negotiations. This is because they were oversold the accomplishments of the Uruguay Round regarding market access and feel that many countries have failed to live up to their agricultural commitments. This has made it difficult for the political system to grant the President the 'fast track' authority needed to conduct meaningful negotiations at a wider Millennium Round. It has also made it difficult for the United States to come up with a coherent negotiation position. There is agreement within the United States, however, that there should be a complete elimination of export subsidies. As it has few export subsidies, this is a relatively costless demand for the United States to make. Of course, it is in direct opposition to the European Unions' priorities.

The United States also wants stronger rules for STEs which act as export or import monopolies. The Canadian Wheat Board and the New Zealand Dairy Board are important targets but a number of central and eastern European countries and also developing countries retain STEs that could be affected by any tightening of the rules.

In terms of domestic levels of support for farmers, the United States will likely push for the elimination of, or a reduction in, the scope of blue box exemptions, but even this is a contentious internal issue due to current low commodity prices and hence new domestic political pressure requesting support payments.

The United States will likely push for a standard method for establishing TRQs to ensure that whatever levels of access are agreed to are actually realized. Market access for biotechnology is also likely to be an issue for the United States.

3.10.4 Japan

Japan has consistently been a major opponent of agricultural trade liberalization. This is because of concerns over food security in a country with little agricultural land and a large population. As a result, trade barriers have always been high on the major staple – rice – and livestock commodities, but not livestock feed (Kerr et al., 1994). Given the high Japanese levels of support for agriculture, farmland values are now highly capitalized and hence there is this a considerable vested interest in retaining agricultural protection. Further, since the ongoing financial crisis in Japan stems from bad loans made against non-agricultural real estate, it seems unlikely that the Japanese government will allow trade policy changes which would precipitate an agricultural land value crisis. The malaise affecting the Japanese economy shows no signs of abating, with unemployment becoming a reality in Japan for the first time in more than a generation (Yeung, Perdikis and Kerr, 1999). Agriculture has traditionally been a residual employment sector in Japan during periods of economic slowdown and one of the reasons official unemployment has been so low (Kerr et al., 1994). Hence, it also appears unlikely that the Japanese government will concede anything in trade negotiations that would threaten rural employment.

Further, the Japanese make extensive use of tariff escalation – whereby raw materials and low value-added goods enter at low tariff rates while finished products using the same raw materials as inputs have high tariff levels imposed – in the name of encouraging high value-added production and employment in Japan. Regardless of the wisdom of this policy, it remains popular and unlikely to be changed in times of high levels of unemployment by Japanese standards. Hence, tariffs on beef and pork are likely to remain high relative to feed grains.

All of this suggests that the Japanese will fiercely resist further liberalization of agricultural trade. Market access will be kept as restrictive as possible through the use of TRQs and Japan will resist suggestions that reforms are necessary to increase the transparency of their TRQ system.

If there is no general Millennium Round and negotiations are confined to agriculture alone, little progress is likely to be made on the liberalization of the Japanese market. If the negotiations are broad-based, then it may be possible to entice the Japanese to commit to some agricultural liberalization by threatening to withhold concessions in other sectors that the Japanese feel are necessary for their economic recovery.

3.10.5 The Cairns Group

The bloc of non-subsidizing agricultural exporting countries known as the Cairns Group came together before the Uruguay Round to ensure that national agricultural policies would be brought under GATT disciplines. They were largely successful although, as suggested above, full compliance with the WTO remains a goal which has yet to be realized. The current members of the Cairns group are Australia, Argentina, Brazil, Canada, Chile, Colombia, Fiji, Indonesia, Malaysia, New Zealand, Paraguay, the Philippines, South Africa, Thailand and Uruguay.

True to its export orientation, the Cairns Group will push hard for a number of measures to increase market access. Its members will attempt to have the no/low tariff access levels of TRQs increased. They will seek to reduce bound tariffs to the levels actually applied, to prevent countries using tariffs in a way similar to variable levies to increase domestic price stability. They can be expected to attempt to tighten up the list of allowable subsidies (those considered to be in the green box). They will propose that the blue box exemptions be removed and that export subsidies be totally eliminated. They can be expected to act as the conscience of the member states and to use whatever moral leverage that is available in the largely pragmatic realm of trade negotiations. They may be the source of inventive solutions to deadlocks and the proposers of acceptable compromises.

3.10.6 Little Common Ground

From the review of the issues and the positions of the major players, there seems to be little common ground. This suggests that the negotiations will be acrimonious and extended in terms of the unfinished business of the Uruguay Round. A number of new challenges have arisen since the conclusion of the Uruguay Round which may make it even more difficult to reach agreement. The lack of clear-cut resolutions to the differing positions of the major players or the likely timing of conclusions to the negotiations will make it difficult for other countries to develop their negotiation strategies.

3.11 THE POSITION OF CENTRAL EUROPEAN COUNTRIES

The European Union has committed to expansion into central Europe. Accession negotiations are under way with a first group of countries that includes the Czech Republic, Estonia, Hungary, Poland and Slovenia.[6] Negotiations with a second set of countries that includes most of the remainder of the central European nations appear likely to proceed prior to the conclusion of the first round. For both the current 15 members of the European Union, which we shall call the EU15, and the countries of central Europe, these negotiations complicate and are complicated by the WTO negotiations.

Given the size and potential of the central European economies, the desirability of the European Union's expansion to existing members has not been so carefully scrutinized since the debates over British accession. Such a significant expansion of the EU's market will have important ramifications for the distribution of political power and resource allocation within the EU's institutions. For the central European countries, accession will be a major determinant of economic prosperity in the 21st century. It will also help them to secure a place within Europe and to validate commitments to political democracy and a market-oriented economic system. Thus EU accession will mark a major watershed in the transition from the former command system that was dominated by the Soviet Union. The European Union, of course, shares a strong mutual interest in political and economic stability in central Europe, as underlined by conflicts in the Balkans.

Agriculture is perhaps the key area where accession negotiations are likely to be difficult, protracted and possibly acrimonious. One reason for the potential for controversy is the size and potential for growth of the agricultural sectors of countries such as Hungary, Poland and Romania. From the EU perspective, accession of major agricultural nations would subject the CAP to further stress. While the prospect of accession along with existing fiscal pressures, the need to comply with Uruguay Round commitments and the new WTO negotiations have all pushed in the direction of further CAP reform, agricultural vested interests in the European Union have strongly resisted significant reductions in support. The European Union's difficulties in managing these conflicting pressures are reflected in the modest and ambiguous 'Agenda 2000' reforms, which postpone reviews and decisions on a number of important matters, such as milk quotas. With the slow pace and uncertain extent of CAP reform, the accession negotiations as well as the WTO negotiations are made more difficult for the European Union. For the central European countries, much of the growth potential for agriculture depends on obtaining unimpeded access to EU markets and securing the resources that are required to transform the sector technically and organizationally.

Both the European Union and the various central European countries have a large variety of different agriculture policies, which are often applied on a commodity-specific basis. This means that the negotiations will often take place in reference to specific commodities, because harmonization to the CAP will have different producer, trade and budgetary ramifications depending on the mix of policies in question. In some cases, a particular new member will be a winner – in others, a loser. Contrary to popular opinion, there are cases where the European Union will be a winner. In assessing the impact of accession, both computational general equilibrium analysis and individual market studies will be essential. For the latter studies, the techniques developed in Chapter 2 remain directly applicable.

The three principle channels through which accession will affect welfare in central European countries are budgetary transfers, producer price effects and consumer price effects. Since direct contributions to the European Union budget are income related and since the central European countries are relatively poor, net support payments to agriculture and other programme spending will typically outweigh the direct contributions the acceding countries will make to the European Union and confer a net budgetary benefit. While it should be noted that 90 per cent of tariff revenue must be turned over to Brussels, the central European countries will escape financial responsibility for CAP export subsidies and domestic support measures. Since domestic producer prices in the agricultural sector tend to be higher in the European Union than in the central European countries, there will tend to be producer gains. However, these overall gains will not be universal. For example, while producer prices in Poland are generally lower than in the European Union, the reverse is true in some important sectors such as poultry and pork production. Juxtaposed against the overall budgetary and producer gains are possible consumer losses. In many but by no means all markets, the domestic market prices facing consumers in central European countries will rise upon accession.

The impact of accession on the European Union arises primarily through the budgetary channel. The issues pertaining to budgetary aspects of the CAP have both disbursement and revenue-raising aspects. Where acceding countries are eligible for domestic support such as headage or acreage payments under the CAP, additional EU outlays will obviously be required. The impact on the EU budget of trade-related support measures depends on whether the acceding countries import or export after they harmonize with the CAP. When the acceding countries import a particular commodity, there will be an increase in EU net revenue as tariff revenue rises or outlays on export subsidies fall. Contrariwise, when the acceding countries import, there will be a decline in EU net revenue as tariff revenue falls or as outlays on export subsidies rise.[7]

Since the budgetary levies on central European countries will not fully compensate for net expenditures on programmes at current intervention levels, accession would lead to induced minor reductions in EU intervention levels for some commodities due to budget ceilings that are built into the current CAP. Such automatic adjustments will generate benefits to consumers and damages to producers in the EU15. Further, there will be secondary budgetary changes that must be beneficial to Brussels for all commodities that the EU15 had been exporting and that could also be beneficial for some imported commodities depending on elasticities of supply and demand. In all cases, these secondary effects have a strong tendency to be beneficial because they are trade liberalizing and move the European Union closer to world prices. Although EU15 producers may be expected to strongly object to, and lobby forcefully against, such a budget-constrained decline in support, the institutional structure of the EU15 is such that the accession will cause secondary gains to the EU15 as a whole.

Neither the budgetary implications nor the reductions to farm sector support in the EU15 are politically palatable. Further, the European Union's budgetary ability to respond is limited by its Uruguay Round WTO commitments and may be limited further by the current WTO negotiations on agriculture. In these circumstances, possible EU strategies include drawing out the negotiating process, establishing long phase-in periods for agriculture and/or limiting the participation of new members in CAP programmes. While limits on access to markets are likely to take the form of phased liberalization over time, limits on production and access to EU funds may be of a more permanent nature.

If world prices were to remain constant, there would be joint gains to the EU15 and new members only on those markets where EU intervention levels were initially lower and enlargement trade liberalizing. As we have seen such market configurations tend to be the exception rather than the rule. This suggests that, from a narrow economic standpoint, accession is not likely to be a 'win–win' situation in the short run and emphasizes that the negotiations will be difficult. As trade is diverted within the enlarged European Union, however, world prices will tend to move in favour of the European Union acting as a source of joint gains. Historic experience also suggests that the enlarged European Union is likely to experience dynamic trade creation gains as the economy and the agricultural sector grow more rapidly than would otherwise have been the case. Outside trade partners would tend to be harmed by trade diversion but gain from dynamic trade creation. Trade creation and trade diversion are discussed further in Chapter 4.

The timing of accession poses some interesting issues for central European countries and, interestingly enough, may provide some common ground with the EU15. While the EU process of CAP reform, the accession negotiations and the WTO negotiations are all likely to be protracted, it is conceivable that some central European countries may accede to the European Union prior to the completion of the WTO negotiations and with further CAP reform still looming. In such a case, producers of many agricultural products in central Europe may be exposed to temporarily high support levels that erode with the conclusion of the WTO negotiations and further CAP reform. This would lead to overadjustment of supply in the short run. Such overadjustment is a problem, not only because adjustment is costly but also because vested interests would be created that would resist CAP reform. To avoid overadjustment, a staged incorporation into the CAP may actually be in the interest of the acceding countries as well as the EU15. If this common interest is recognized and tapped, the accession negotiations could proceed somewhat more smoothly.

Accession may also pose problems with respect to the existing WTO commitments for both the European Union and its new members. For those commodities where the acceding countries must raise tariffs above bound levels to harmonize with the common trade policy of the European Union, they will be in breach of their WTO commitments. Under WTO rules, trading partners may seek compensation or impose retaliatory measures if compensation is not paid. If these matters cannot be resolved through negotiation and if the trading partners are able to obtain an affirmative ruling from a WTO disputes panel, then retaliation rather than compensation may be the lesser of two evils for the new EU members and, indeed, the European Union itself. Compensation is based on the gross value of the export revenue that the complainant would have received if the tariff had not been increased. When a complainant retaliates, it can reduce its imports from the defendant on commodities of its choice up to the same value. Despite appearances, the real costs of compensation and retaliation are not the same. When the complainant retaliates, the defendant is forced to move the resources that would have been employed in producing exports for the complainant into the next-best available use but these resources are not lost entirely. In an extreme case where the same product is diverted to alternative export markets at the same world price, there is no cost at all, other than the transaction cost of making the switch in markets.

Under the provisions of the URAA, similar problems may arise for commodities in which the acceding countries increase their net exports as a result of harmonizing with the CAP. For such commodities, combined outlays on export subsidies will rise, making it more difficult for the expanded European Union to achieve its Uruguay Round commitments on reducing export subsidies. If these commitments cannot be met, the enlarged European Union may ultimately face the choice of paying compensation or accepting retaliation. Once again, it is better to accept retaliation.

From the perspective of the central European countries that are negotiating accession, the simultaneous WTO negotiations represent a mixed blessing. In Section 3.3, we saw that there is pressure from various quarters to remove the so-called 'water in the tariff' by reducing bound tariff rates to actual rates. For countries such as Poland that have administered TRQs on an applied tariff basis where the TRQ-quota has been ignored (see Section 3.2), this would reduce the bound tariff to the within-quota tariff. If the WTO negotiations move more rapidly than the accession negotiations, those central European countries that have kept their bound tariffs high to facilitate eventual entry into the European Union will have to be on their guard against such reductions in bound tariffs. Otherwise, there could be a marked increase in the degree to which compensation or retaliation becomes a problem upon accession. As argued in Section 3.3, it would be bad trade politics to punish those countries that went beyond their required Uruguay Round commitments by administering their actual tariffs at below the maximum allowable rates.

The WTO negotiations also represent an opportunity for central European countries. As independent parties, the central European countries are free to suggest alternatives and affect the WTO negotiations in their own interest. They would not be able to do this if they were already in the European Union or had adopted a common negotiating strategy. The central European countries, allied with other outside countries, may also have a more profound influence over reform of the CAP through the WTO negotiations than they could, independently or collectively, either during or after the accession negotiations.

The issues of market access and domestic subsidies, which are at the heart of the negotiations surrounding the accessions of central European countries to the European Union, are all part of the 'unfinished business' of the Uruguay Round. There are, however, a large number of issues that have arisen in agricultural trade since the completion of the Uruguay Round. Some old issues that were 'swept under the carpet' at the Uruguay Round have gained new prominence. It is to these 'new' issues that we turn in Chapter 4.

NOTES

1. The Uruguay Round also addressed some key NTBs beyond the agricultural sector. Since the 1960s, world trade in textiles and clothing had been managed through a multilateral system of trade quotas known as the Multi-Fibre Arrangements (MFAs). Further, throughout the1980s in sectors such as automobiles and steel, importing countries frequently insisted that their trade partners *voluntarily* limit exports. These quantitative restrictions on exports were known as voluntary export restraints (VERs). The Uruguay Round Agreement prohibits VERs, and is gradually moving textiles and apparel back into the regular GATT system by converting quotas into tariffs.

2. If the government gave domestic food aid to any consumers who would have purchased wheat at the home market price of Ph, demand would be reduced on a one-for-one basis and the excess supply of wheat would not be reduced.

3. Other allegedly de-coupled subsidies, such as subsidies to research and development, typically have similar effects on long-run entry or exit decisions. Thus few if any subsidies are fully de-coupled from output in the long run.

4. Interestingly enough, if the country is initially exporting, the milk quotas could be welfare improving for the domestic economy. Since the quota rents will be partially paid by foreigners, the increase in quota rents could outweigh the loss of domestic consumer surplus. Foreigners, of course, would face an overall welfare reduction; foreign consumers would lose more than foreign producers would gain.

5. A 'normal' rate of return is considered part of the user cost of capital (the payment required to keep investment in the firm) by economists and thus is part of the long-run average cost, $LACb$.

6. The Mediterranean island nation of Malta is also in the first group being considered for EU accession.

7. Whether the EU15 imports or exports does not matter directly. It is only through induced changes in world prices that the trade status of the EU15 might affect its post-accession budgetary position.

4. New challenges

4.1 HEALTH, SANITARY AND PHYTO-SANITARY RULES FOR TRADE

As formal barriers to the trade in goods have come down through successive rounds of GATT negotiations, non-border methods of distorting trade have become of increasing concern to those who formulate trade policy. The increasing concern over non-border measures that have trade effects has arisen for two reasons. First, in the era of high tariffs, countries were able to enact a large number of legitimate domestic regulations in their isolated markets. While these regulations had no trade-distorting intent, as tariffs were removed, exporters began to have to deal with domestic regulation which inhibited their ability to access markets. Second, as border measures were removed and could not be re-imposed due to WTO commitments, countries began to design and administer domestic regulations in a purposeful manner to limit the access of foreign goods when faced with pressure from protectionists.

One area that was perceived as being particularly open to trade-distorting domestic regulations, either by accident or by design, was regulatory regimes dealing with human, animal and plant health. Further, as a large proportion of the products covered by these types of regulation had their origin in agricultural production, there was heightened scepticism regarding the innocence of trade-distorting regulations. Agriculture, due to the waivers it enjoyed, had high levels of border measures and high rates of subsidization long after trade barriers had been considerably reduced in most other sectors. It was only reluctantly brought under WTO disciplines at the Uruguay Round, and agricultural lobbies remain strong. As a result, it was expected that governments would be under considerable pressure to find ways to continue to extend protection to agriculture. As the regulations concerning human, animal and plant health were, in many cases, implemented by ministries of agriculture (which are often perceived as being captured by farm interests) and not under the jurisdiction of international trade ministries, ample opportunities for potential abuse were present (Kerr, 1997).

As a result, at the Uruguay Round a new Agreement on the Application of Sanitary and Phyto-sanitary Measures (SPS) was negotiated. It applies to regulations pertaining to human health, animal health and plant health ('phyto' means pertaining to plants). All aspects of the agri-food chain are covered, including food safety, health of animals issues affecting both humans and other animals, and both plant diseases and the use of substances such as herbicides and pesticides. While the SPS deals extensively with agriculture-related issues, it was not part of the Uruguay Round Agreement on Agriculture (URAA) and hence not slated for the automatic resumption in the negotiations in 2000. However, a number of high-profile disputes brought to the WTO under the SPS since the Uruguay Round and the looming spectre of regulating trade in genetically modified foods have led to calls for the SPS to be opened for re-negotiation.

The issues surrounding food safety and other aspects of a nation's health security are complex. Protecting the health and safety of citizens is seen as a fundamental role for governments. Countries guard their sovereignty in these areas very carefully. On a practical political level, there can be few more damaging events than a breakdown in the food safety system, both for the government currently in power and individual political careers. It does not matter to the public if the food safety breach occurred in a far-away processing plant in another country; it is their domestic government which is responsible for their welfare. As a result, it is not easy to persuade governments to give up sovereignty to international organizations in this area of public policy and they may be more willing to snatch it back when there is a perceived threat. National governments of EU countries were, for example, quick to re-exercise sovereignty in contravention to EU agreements and impose trade barriers against British beef during the 'mad cow disease' crisis.

The areas of domestic regulation covered by the SPS are extensive and include food production, processing, handling, inspecting and testing. Individual countries have independently developed their regulations in these areas. Even small differences in, for example, testing procedures can lead to foreign products being excluded from a market. Scientific training and traditions vary among countries. Those establishing domestic food safety regulations assume that their methods and ways of doing things are the best – after all if they were not then they would not have been doing their jobs. Foreign standards are often regarded with suspicion. It is also easy to see how subtle differences in regulations that provide the same degree of food safety can be used purposefully as trade barriers.

The SPS is subject to some general WTO principles. Domestic regulations must not discriminate among foreign suppliers – the same regulations should apply to all members of the WTO. The regulations applied to foreign suppliers should not be more stringent than those that apply to domestic producers. The regulations should be transparent so that those wishing to export into the market can take measures to satisfy the regulations. If two methods of regulation can achieve the same level of food safety, then the one that imposes the lower compliance cost should be used. Within these broad principles, however, there is ample scope for abuse of health, sanitary and phyto-sanitary regulations as trade barriers. As a result, the SPS goes further in specifying the nature of domestic regulations.

There must be a scientific basis for the regulations put in place. This is to prevent the imposition of regulations that have no safety-enhancing value, yet impose costs on foreign firms wishing to access the market. Further, countries must undertake a risk assessment to justify the imposition of a regulation. This is meant to prevent the putting in place of costly regulations which, while they have a scientific basis, actually protect against problems with an insignificant level of risk. All food safety procedures are based (explicitly or implicitly) on the scientific method and statistical probabilities. It is not possible to guarantee absolute safety. In recognition that different societies may have different risk thresholds, countries are allowed to establish their own levels of risk. The WTO appears to interpret this to mean that countries cannot be inconsistent in the levels of risk that they apply – in other words they cannot set a different standard of risk for beef produced using hormones, for example, than that used for other food safety procedures (Roberts, 1998).

One means of dealing with differences between national regulations would be for countries to grant equivalence to foreign regulations and procedures if they deliver the same level of safety. As discussed above, given the egocentric nature of those who develop national regulations, this has proved very difficult. In a similar fashion, in areas of human capital such as the training of veterinarians and food inspectors, 'national treatment' whereby foreign-trained personnel are treated as if they are domestic nationals would provide a means to eliminate regulatory barriers to trade. Again, this route has not been particularly effective owing to professional jealousies and difficulties in determining whether standards are similar and will continue to be similar. With these less costly methods of removing regulatory barriers to trade having failed to achieve widespread acceptance, the more difficult route of international harmonization is being attempted.

Three international standards organizations that pre-date the SPS have been identified specifically in the agreement and charged with developing harmonized standards. These are, for food safety, the Codex Alimentarius Commission; for animal health, the International Office of Epizootics; and for plant health, the Secretariat of the International Plant Protection Convention. These multilateral organizations remain largely in the realm of individuals with professional or technical expertise. They develop standards, guidelines and other recommendations through long consensus-building negotiations. Slow and careful progress is their hallmark. When one observes the activities of these organizations, it is obvious that *science is not science*. The scientists find it difficult to reach a consensus and their negotiations are protracted. Hence, it seems unlikely that harmonized systems of international regulations for human, animal and plant health will be developed in the near future.

The major test for the SPS provisions since their inception at the conclusion of the Uruguay Round has been the long-standing dispute between the European Union and the United States over the EU's ban on the importation of beef produced using growth hormones. The European Union has refused to license the use of growth-promoting hormones domestically and, to protect the integrity of their market, has also prohibited the importation of beef produced using hormones. These naturally occurring hormones have been licensed for use in cattle production in most beef-producing countries in the world, including the United States and Canada, for decades. The United States and Canada took the case to the WTO disputes settlement system. The WTO found in favour of the United States and Canada. Although the judgement is complex, its essential elements are that the European Union did not provide sufficient scientific evidence that meat from animals produced using growth hormones represents a health risk – it failed the scientific justification test – and that it was applying a risk standard that was inconsistent with other risk standards applied in the European Union (Roberts, 1998).

Thus, the SPS appears to be operating as it was designed to do. It was put in place to prevent the capricious use of, among others, food safety regulations to extend protection to domestic producers. The European Union failed both of the tests established in the SPS – it failed to provide credible scientific evidence to justify its regulations and its application of risk assessment was inconsistent with other EU food safety systems. It has decided not to comply with the WTO ruling and to keep its market closed to beef produced using hormones. It is going to continue its ban and accept retaliation from its trading partners. It is rare for countries to accept retaliation. The threat of retaliation is supposed to keep countries in line. When it is accepted, it suggests a breakdown in the political consensus that underlies the WTO. As suggested in Chapter 1 the WTO is not a legal system – it is a political compromise.

The problem with the hormone case is not that the SPS has failed, it is that the WTO does not recognize any source of protectionist pressure other than domestic producers. In the hormone case, the source of protectionist pressure is EU consumers. Officials in the European Union have had the difficult task of dealing with consumer resistance to having beef produced using hormones in their markets. There is a crisis of confidence regarding the food safety system in the European Union. Sufficient numbers of consumers simply do not trust either food safety officials or the scientific evidence presented. In this case, 'sufficient numbers' means that they cannot easily be ignored by politicians. The ban on hormone use was put in place in response to consumer resistance. Of course, when domestic producers are denied a more efficient technology that is freely available to foreign producers, they will request protection from those foreign producers. Further, in the case of the European Union, the reduced production arising as a result of the unavailability of hormones assisted in the management of Common Agricultural Policy (CAP) beef surpluses. The import ban, hence, assisted in achieving a number of policy goals even though the primary motivation was consumer resistance. The United States has consistently discounted consumer concerns choosing to concentrate on other EU motivations.

The European Union has asked that the SPS agreement be re-opened to take account of consumer preferences. The United States has, rightly, refused to agree. As suggested above, the SPS appears to be operating as expected – it is able to prevent the capricious use of regulations to protect producers. It should probably be left alone. This begs the question of how consumer requests for protection are to be dealt with. In an increasingly complex and affluent world, other groups may ask for protection. Both consumers (Perdikis and Kerr, 1999) and environmentalists (Gordon,

Hannesson and Kerr, 2000) have become active seekers of protection in recent years. The WTO has no means to deal with these new protectionist forces, yet domestic politicians are under intense pressure from both groups to extend protection. The issue of how to deal with consumer resistance to genetically modified foods is also looming and will require urgent attention. The issues surrounding genetically modified foods are dealt with in more detail later in this Chapter. While the SPS deals with food safety issues, it seems ill-designed to deal with consumer (and environmentalist) concerns that are based largely on questions where information is incomplete or that are due to a distrust of the scientific establishment (Perdikis and Kerr, 1999). These issues must be dealt with at the WTO but the SPS may not be the appropriate venue.

4.2 TECHNICAL BARRIERS TO TRADE

Technical barriers to trade have become more prominent in the minds of trade policy makers in recent decades. The barriers to trade, discussed in Section 4.1, that are regulated under the SPS agreement are technical barriers to trade. The political importance of health and sanitary issues and the unique set of biologically based problems that dealing with live or perishable organisms presents, suggested that they required a special set of rules. Other technical barriers to trade are regulated under a GATT subagreement titled the Agreement on Technical Barriers to Trade (TBT). As with the SPS barriers, the types of trade barriers covered by the TBT have become more prominent as border measures have been reduced or removed. Domestic regulations of many types can inhibit international trade and are open to abuses in regulatory design and administration.

The TBT is important for agriculture because it applies to domestic regulations on food, agricultural production and agricultural inputs that do not directly concern food safety, animal health or plant health. The most obvious examples are regulations to protect consumers from fraud, such as labelling a product as beef when it is actually goat. Even here, protection from fraud may have food safety considerations if individuals who are allergic to goat have their health put at risk by inaccurate labelling.

The TBT applies general WTO principles to the design and administration of domestic technical regulations that affect imported goods. The regulations should not violate the WTO principle of non-discrimination; that is, the regulations should be applied to the products of all WTO member states equally. They should be no more rigorous for foreign firms than for domestic firms. The regulations should be transparent so that foreign suppliers are able to take steps to comply with the regulations.

One of the areas where the TBT is applied that affects the trade in agricultural commodities relates to a consumer's right to be informed. This applies both to contents labelling and the language of labelling. Exporters may be required to provide labels in the language(s) of the importing country. Ingredient or nutritional information may be required on packaging. Health and safety warnings may be required on imported agricultural chemicals.

The consumer's right to know can extend to information on how a product was produced. Exporters may be required to provide information on whether pesticides were used in production, whether growth hormones were used or whether animals were produced in a welfare-friendly fashion. Note, however, that trade barriers cannot be put in place based on the processes used in production.

While all these information issues are legitimate concerns, the way domestic regulations are constituted can be used as a means to protect domestic producers from foreign competition and hence become a technical barrier to trade. These domestic regulations can become a barrier to trade in a number of ways. First, they may add directly to the cost of production. For example, if labelling requirements differ between countries, then new labels often have to be designed and then approved by the importing country, which can cause lengthy delays. Each time a product designated for export is produced, the production line may have to be shut down while alternative labels are integrated into the process. The requirement that consumers in an importing country be allowed to visually inspect the product in the package may require new packaging, or even new machinery if a similar regulation does not exist in the home market. Regulations requiring imports to be in standardized package sizes rather than available in bulk may require exporters to invest in new and expensive product-handling equipment.

Second, proving the claims made on labels may be very costly for a foreign firm. For example, let us say that a firm in a country without an organic certification programme sees an opportunity to profitably access a foreign market for organic products. It may be easy to put an organic label on a product but how does one prove to authorities in the importing country that it was organically produced, that it wasn't mixed with non-organic products during processing or transport and that it was not contaminated with chemicals. Proof requires expensive 'identity preservation' systems to be put in place.

Third, meeting the multiple standards of different countries may not be feasible, forcing firms to choose among export markets. If one country requires that cold pasteurization be used in food processing while another bans it entirely, it may not be possible for a firm that wishes to export to simultaneously satisfy both sets of regulations. If standards for meat-processing buildings differ among countries, facilities tailored to one export market may be required.

Recognizing the costs that different standards can impose on exporters, the TBT promotes the adoption of international standards such as ISO and hazard analysis–critical control points (HACCP). While the HACCP is strictly speaking, an international standard designed to improve food safety, the HACCP experience is illustrative of the difficulties associated with adopting international standards.

The first major international organization to advocate HACCP was the World Health Organisation (WHO) in the early 1970s. The use of HACCP was not officially recommended internationally until 1983. In that year it received the endorsement of the joint food safety committee of the UN's Food and Agriculture Organization (FAO) and the WHO. It was not until 1993 that the Codex Alimentarius Commission agreed that the HACCP system was the most cost-effective approach devised to date for ensuring the safety of food.

While a significant achievement, this 25 year process has yielded far less than true international harmonization. The Codex Guidelines for Application of HACCP contain ambiguities that allow conflicting interpretations of the HACCP system, thereby throwing up impediments to the harmonization of food safety regulations. There are major disagreements over what an international HACCP system should contain. There are also disagreements over the scientific elements of food safety, whether HACCP should be mandatory and what would constitute independent verification.

The technical barriers to trade that arise in the absence of international harmonization to HACCP are considerable. The lack of agreement over standards allows 'first jump' countries to insist that their standards be met before a product can enter their market. This may impose standards that are nearly impossible for less technically capable countries to meet. It may also allow unique domestic standards to be captured by protectionist interests and used for their own objectives. If, for example, a country's version of HACCP requires specific investments to achieve compliance, after having made those investments, it may be possible for firms to convince domestic policy makers to delay the adoption of international standards until their capital has been fully depreciated. They may also be able to create doubts about the relative efficacy of the international and the domestic standard and thus delay the former's adoption. The domestic firms will, all the while, enjoy the protection imparted by the domestic standard and its specialized investment requirements.

Hence, relying on harmonization as the means to remove technical barriers to trade is fraught with difficulties. Of course, the central problem is that most technical barriers to trade have a genuine domestic basis for their imposition. It is very difficult to distinguish between a genuine regulation and one put in place simply to extend protection to domestic producers that lobby for it. In the case of technical barriers to trade, it is not even possible to examine the scientific justification for the regulation or to insist on a risk assessment.

In recognition of these difficulties, the negotiators of the TBT have taken a different approach in their attempt to control the capricious use of technical requirements. Enshrined in the TBT, but as yet untested at the WTO, is the principle that the cost of complying with domestic regulations for foreign firms must be proportional to the purpose of the standard. This means, for example, that the costs imposed on exporters in complying with food-labelling requirements should not exceed the benefits consumers receive from having the information on the label.

The implicit cost–benefit analysis enshrined in the TBT may lead to disagreement over how to measure the consumer benefits arising from labelling or other regulations. This issue may become more contentious if, instead of attempting to exclude products from their markets directly, countries choose to use labelling instead. The beef hormone and genetically modified foods issues would appear to be two where this policy response might be expected. In both cases, verifying labels may require expensive identity preservation systems to be put in place. Exporters may argue that the costs exceed the benefits which consumers receive. Arriving at a consensus on the benefits to consumers will not be easy.

The URAA allowed for what are euphemistically referred to as 'non-trade' issues to be on the agenda at the talks slated for 2000. Some countries, particularly Scandinavian ones, have been pushing the issue of animal welfare. They wish to restrict the import of animal products because of the costs imposed on their producers by more stringent domestic regulations. While the TBT does not have to be re-opened in the current negotiations, the issue of animal welfare-friendly production might be better dealt with within the TBT.

Thus, significant agricultural issues such as genetically modified foods and animal welfare may lead to pressure to have the TBT re-opened for negotiation. If it is, these agricultural issues will be high on the agenda.

4.3 THE PROTECTION OF INTELLECTUAL PROPERTY

The development and application of new technologies and new products has been central to the development of the agricultural sector and the economy in general. Technological development poses the question of whether the ideas and information generated by research and development (R & D) and other creative activity can be owned in the same way as physical assets. The notion of 'intellectual property' essentially extends the definition of property and ownership to encompass ideas, inventions and creative expression (Sherwood, 1990). Governments often act, individually or collectively, to uphold the ownership of new ideas by conferring intellectual property rights. Patents, copyrights and trademarks are the three most prominent means of protecting intellectual property. Patents protect new products or production processes by preventing other individuals or firms from unlicensed production or use for the duration of the patent. Similarly, copyrights protect literary works, music, art and now software from unlicensed reproduction for the duration of the copyright. Trademarks provide for the exclusive use of the names and symbols of firms, products and so on. While copyrights and patents last for a fixed duration and are non-renewable, trademarks can be renewed in perpetuity. Other forms of intellectual property protection include geographic indicators (for example, champagne wine must come from the Champagne area in France), industrial designs and protection of trade secrets.

Intellectual property protection is both important and controversial in the agri-food sector where the application of new technology has long been prominent. While earlier waves of innovation, including the 'green revolution' technologies of the 1960s and 1970s, have often posed important socio-economic issues, they have not been particularly contentious on intellectual property grounds. For example, the development and application of pesticides, herbicides and fertilizers have often been, and continue to be, very controversial from an environmental perspective, but not from an intellectual property perspective. Modern developments in biotechnology have completely changed this. In addition to potential environmental and health concerns and the ethical issue of tampering with genes, which are discussed further in the following sections, genetic engineering brings to the forefront the ethical issue of owning and patenting life forms.

At the outset, it is necessary to ask why governments bestow intellectual property rights. The ideas and information that arise from creative activity in general and R & D in particular are similar in economic respects to 'public goods' such as national defence. Public goods are 'non-rivalrous' and 'non-excludable'. A new technology is non-rivalrous in the sense that any firm can make use of it without detracting from the simultaneous use of it by other firms. Use of information by one firm does not preclude use by others, as with private goods. A new technology is non-excludable in that it would be difficult, costly and often ultimately impossible to prevent other producers from using it in the absence of intellectual property protection by governments. Public goods lead to a 'free-rider' problem. In the case of a new technology, each producer has the incentive to free-ride on the innovations of its rivals because copying a technology (for example, through the use of reverse engineering) is typically much less costly than performing the original R & D. This dramatically reduces the incentive to invest in R & D in the first place.

The protection of intellectual property is a partial or 'second best' solution to the problem of underinvestment in R & D. Patents and copyrights, for example, afford a temporary monopoly whereby an innovating firm becomes the exclusive user of the technology. While the temporary monopoly increases the incentive to invest in new technologies, it does so by introducing a new distortion. In order to maximize profit a monopoly will supply less than the efficient output. Thus, there is a trade-off: the longer the duration of the patent or copyright, the smaller the underinvestment problem relating to innovation but the larger the undersupply problem relating to production.

The trade-off arising from intellectual property rights can be illustrated using Figure 4.1. The demand curve, *D*, shows the price associated with each quantity of a new product and the marginal revenue curve, *MR*, shows the extra or marginal revenue obtained from selling an additional unit of the product. Marginal revenue is always below price (that is, the *MR* curve lies below the D curve) because the monopolist bids the price down against itself by selling an extra unit. The firm must engage in costly R & D prior to the commencement of production, but these costs are sunk and unchangeable by the time production occurs. Total production costs, however, vary with output. For simplicity, the production costs per unit of output (that is, the marginal and average costs of production) are assumed to be constant and equal to P^*, as shown by the MC, AC curve in Figure 4.1.

First, suppose that there is no patent protection for the new product and that the product can be copied instantaneously without cost. If one firm were to develop the new product, it would lose all of its R & D costs as other firms enter and produce the competitive quantity Q^* and sell at the competitive price P^*. In this extreme case, there would be no R & D at all because no firm would be the first to innovate. Nevertheless, the innovation is socially beneficial provided that the present value of the consumer surplus of $a + \ldots + e$ dollars in perpetuity exceeds the costs of R & D. Even allowing for costly, non-instantaneous reverse engineering, less than the efficient level of R & D will be forthcoming.

Now suppose that patent protection is introduced so that an innovating firm will be a monopoly for a limited time after innovation. Under monopoly, the innovating firm will maximize profit by producing Qm, where the marginal revenue just covers the marginal cost of the last unit of output produced. Since the firm will charge a price of Pm, its revenue will exceed its production costs by $c + d$ dollars. Provided that the present value of $c + d$ dollars over the life of the patent is greater than or equal to the initial outlays on R & D, the firm's overall profit will be greater than or equal to zero and investment in R & D will proceed. Clearly, there will be a greater incentive to invest in R & D the longer is the duration of patent protection. Nevertheless, even if patents last forever, innovation would not reach the fully efficient level. Innovation, while socially beneficial if the present value of $a + \ldots + e$ per period exceeds R & D costs, would not proceed if R & D costs exceeded the present value of $c + d$ dollars per period.

Since the monopolist receives $c + d$ dollars per period and the new consumer surplus is equal to $a + b$ dollars per period, the total surplus is $a + \ldots + d$ dollars per period over the life of the patent. While this is clearly better than nothing at all, it remains inefficient. After the patent expires and

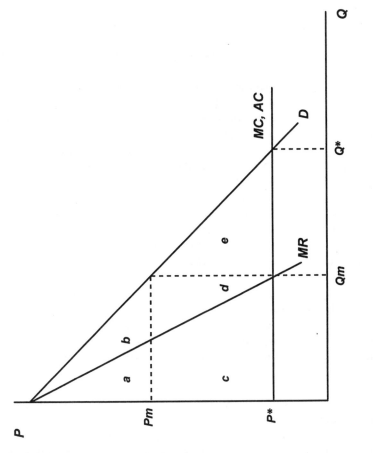

Figure 4.1: Product innovation

139

other firms enter, industry output will rise to Q^*, the price will fall to P^* and consumers surplus and total surplus will increase to $a + \ldots + e$ dollars per period. Thus, there is an efficiency loss associated with a monopoly of e dollars per period over the duration of the patent. While a longer duration of patent protection reduces underinvestment in R & D, it increases the efficiency loss from monopoly.

There is an important international dimension to the issue of intellectual property protection. Each country has an incentive to free-ride on the intellectual property protection of other countries and avoid the efficiency losses associated with temporary monopoly in its own market. Thus each country will tend to provide low levels of intellectual property and/or offer lax enforcement of those measures that are in place. In either case, the incentive for firms to invest in R & D will be diminished; in the latter case, pirate firms are likely to enter the market and produce without acquiring licences or paying royalties. Further, enforcement is likely to be discriminatory as well as lax, with governments affording greater levels of effective intellectual property protection to domestic innovating firms.

Attempts to deal with the international issues concerning intellectual property protection have a long history. The Paris Convention of 1883 initiated a degree of international cooperation on patents and the Berne convention of 1886 did the same for copyrights. A coordinating body, the World Intellectual Property Organization (WIPO) was founded in 1967. Unfortunately, these efforts at cooperation and coordination on intellectual property protection lacked minimum standards and any effective mechanisms to ensure enforcement and settle disputes. As the comparative advantage of developed countries, and especially the United States, became increasingly dependent on advanced, knowledge-based products, and as the pace of technological development accelerated in the latter decades of the 20th century, the lack of effective intellectual property protection in many countries became a trade issue.

In the Uruguay Round negotiations, the United States, backed by most developed countries, vigorously advocated for, and obtained, an Agreement on Trade-Related Aspects of Intellectual Property Rights (TRIPS), against the wishes of many developing countries. All WTO members are required to adopt the TRIPS, which augments rather than subsumes the earlier international agreements. Developed countries were given a one-year implementation period, developing countries and countries in transition from command to market-based systems were given five years, and the least developed countries were given 11 years. Further, the operation of the Agreement itself was made subject to review after five years.

The TRIPS imposes world minimum standards of 20 years for the duration of patents and 50 years for copyrights. Countries may choose, however, whether or not to allow patents on life forms. The Agreement embraces 'national treatment' whereby foreign and domestic firms are treated symmetrically. While each country can choose its own enforcement procedures, these must be effective and transparent. Intellectual property disputes can be taken before regular WTO panels. Further, if a country is found to be in contravention of its commitments and will not desist and/or pay compensation, other countries can take retaliatory action. Such retaliation may take place within the TRIPS agreement but, if that is not practicable, cross-agreement retaliation is permitted. Thus, if Thailand did not properly protect the intellectual property of US firms, the US government could take trade actions limiting the importation of Thai goods under the GATT.

In spite of the need for cooperation on intellectual property rights protection to prevent nations from free-riding, there are some serious problems with the TRIPS. There is undoubtedly a degree of economic elegance to the symmetric world standards for patents and copyrights because protection everywhere expires at approximately the same time. Nevertheless, it is hard to reconcile the symmetric standards of intellectual property protection with the asymmetric pattern of benefits where most of the monopoly profits and other producer benefits accrue to developed as opposed to developing countries. Further, these symmetric levels of intellectual property protection are at odds with longstanding GATT traditions. While tariffs have traditionally been subject to symmetric cuts, there has certainly never been a requirement for symmetry in tariff levels across countries or goods.

While modest and suitably enforced increases in intellectual property protection by all countries have the potential to be mutually beneficial, it appears that the move to world standards will be detrimental to many if not most developing countries (Gaisford and Richardson, 1994). This makes the prospects for enforcement problematic at best in spite of the mechanisms in the TRIPS (Yampoin and Kerr, 1998). In fact, the prospects for enforcement in developing countries are even weaker than they first appear, because the marketing behaviour of innovating foreign firms will depend in part on enforcement. For example, stricter enforcement is not only costly in itself but will also lead to higher royalties being assessed by foreign firms

Table 4.1 Pre-WTO intellectual property protection: selected countries, 1992

Country	Membership	Patents	Copyrights
Argentina	W, B, P	10	+50
Australia	B, P	16	+50
Austria	W, B, P	20	+70
Belgium	W, B, P	20	+50
Brazil	W, B, P	15	+60
Canada	W, B, P	20	+50
Cayman Is.	n.a.	SAO	+50
Chile	W, B, P	15	+30
Columbia	W, B	15	+80
Costa Rica	W, B	12	+50
Cyprus	W, B, P	UK	+50
Denmark	W, B, P	20	+50
Ecuador	W	15	+50
Egypt	W, B, P	15	n.a.
Finland	W, B, P	20	+50
France	W, B, P	20	+50
Germany	W, B, P	20	+70
Greece	W, B, P	20	+50
Guatemala	W	15	n.a.
Hong Kong	B, P	SAO	n.a.
India	W, B	n.a.	+50
Ireland	W, B, P	20	50
Israel	W, B, P	20	+70
Italy	W, B, P	20	+50
Jamaica	n.a.	14	+50
Japan	W, B, P	20	+50
Korea	W, P	15	+50
Luxembourg	W, B, P	20	+50
Malaysia	W, B, P	15	+50
Mexico	B, P	20	+50
Netherlands	W, B, P	20	+50
New Zealand	W, B, P	16	+50
Norway	W, B, P	20	+50
Panama	W	15	n.a.

Country	Membership	Patents	Copyright
Paraguay	W, B	15	+50
Peru	W, B	15	+50
Philippines	W, B, P	17	+50
Portugal	W, B, P	15	+50
Singapore	W	UK	+50
South Africa	W, B, P	20	+50
Spain	W, B, P	20	+60
Switzerland	W, B, P	20	+50
Taiwan	n.a.	n.a.	+50
Thailand	W, B	20	+50
Trinidad	W, B, P	14	n.a.
United Kingdom	W, B, P	20	+50
United States	W, B, P	17	+50
Venezuela	W, B	15	n.a.

Key:
W = World Intellectual Property Organization, B = Berne Convention, P = Paris Convention.
+50, etc. : life of author plus number of years (e.g., 50) of protection.
SAO: patent length is same as in original country.
UK: United Kingdom patent required.
n.a. : Information not available.
Source: Gaisford and Richardson (1994). Information originally compiled and assembled from Hemnes, Dimambo and Moore (1992).

and reduced consumer surplus for the developing country (Tarvydas et al., 1999). These indirect effects reduce the enforcement incentives. Table 4.1 suggests that, by the conclusion of the Uruguay Round, a number of developing countries had already increased their standards, but not necessarily their enforcement effort. While the possibility of retaliation introduced in the TRIPS will go some way toward encouraging enforcement, it is ironic that the higher standards themselves increase the benefits of, and incentives for, piracy.

Now that the five-year implementation period permitted for most developing countries has elapsed, it seems likely that piracy and enforcement will become increasingly contentious. Both developed countries and developing countries may become increasingly frustrated with the TRIPS, albeit for different reasons. The tensions over intellectual property protection in agriculture are likely to become particularly acute. In addition to the enforcement question, the current flexibility permitted on the question of patents on life forms makes for ambiguity and uncertainty in the degree of protection that will be afforded to biotech innovation. The United States is likely to push to close perceived loopholes so that its biotech multinationals have greater assurance their that investments in genetically modified organisms will be protected. Developing countries are likely to resist such a reduction in access to technology, while the European Union may favour the status quo due to public concerns over the technology itself. The following three sections address further issues posed by biotechnology.

4.4   THE COMPLEX ISSUE OF BIOTECHNOLOGY

Biotechnology, in its various manifestations, has the potential to become the defining issue in agricultural trade in the early years of the new millennium. The issues surrounding biotechnology are likely to lead to extremely acrimonious disputes at the WTO (Kerr, 1999). The issues have the potential to severely test the WTO's relatively new and untried institutions. They may threaten the political consensus that underpins the WTO and be the catalyst for major re-negotiations of existing agreements.

Biotechnology represents a significant technological change in agriculture and will be at least equal in importance and effect to the two other major technological changes in the sector that proceeded it: mechanization and applied agro-chemistry. As with any technological change, it will create winners and losers. In part, who wins and who loses will be determined by changes in the terms of trade. In addition, a major and rapid technological change brings with it resistance to change among some segments of the population. Along with potential benefits, biotechnology brings a degree of uncertainty and new risks. Trade liberalization never does well during periods of disequilibrium such as the one which describes the current situation in agricultural biotechnology.

The major stakeholders in this new technology are large transnational agribusiness firms. They have gambled heavily on the potential returns to biotechnology. The pace of change, however, is very rapid and the window for capturing returns on R & D in any product is narrow. Those investing in biotechnology require access to the widest possible market if they are to have a reasonable chance at reaping the expected returns from their investments. Thus the firms investing in the development of agricultural products embodying biotechnology see their operations directly threatened by trade restrictions.

The processes underlying biotechnology are knowledge based. As a result, there are significant intellectual property issues surrounding its diffusion (Kerr, Hobbs and Yampoin, 1999). As suggested in the previous section, the new and untested TRIPS agreement may not be sufficiently robust to provide the international protection expected by those investing in biotechnology (Tarvydas et al., 1999).

The European Union and the United States are in conflict over the access of US biotechnology products to European markets. The longstanding animosity and distrust over agricultural issues between these two major economic powers has left neither side with much sympathy for the other's position. While EU politicians attempt to deal with the difficulties surrounding consumer resistance to products embodying biotechnology, US politicians are faced with demands from their major agribusiness firms that access be assured.

There are also important potential environmental ramifications to the adoption of agricultural biotechnology that have not yet been adequately addressed (Mooney and Klein, 1999). As a result, environmental interests are lobbying for protection from having imported biotechnology products released into their local ecosystems.

As with any new technology, the initial disequilibrium period is characterized by incomplete and asymmetric information. As a result, it is difficult for policy makers, including trade policy makers, to be sure that they are making correct decisions. Given poor information, strong vested interests, issues such as food safety and the environment, and the involvement of transnational corporations, where some individuals have strong (and often loudly voiced) preferences, it is not surprising that the subject of biotechnology has the potential to become a major trade issue.

As with any new phenomenon, there may be confusion over terminology. 'Genetically modified' foods are found under the broad umbrella of biotechnology. Genetic modification refers to the use of modern techniques of genetic enhancement to allow the improvement of biological organisms beyond that which is attainable using natural selection and controlled breeding. There are two types of genetic modification, within-species modification and transgenic modification. Within-species genetic modification uses biotechnological techniques (a process) to accomplish effectively, precisely and quickly what traditional scientific breeding has attempted to do by slow, hit-and-miss methods. As within-species genetic modification simply involves the speeding up of improvements that could be accomplished using more traditional breeding procedures. there are already many genetically modified food products on supermarket shelves. These products have experienced little consumer resistance except when confused with transgenic products, which also fit within the broader category of genetically modified foods.

Transgenics, or more precisely, trans-species genetic modification, differs from traditional breeding in that it enables gene transfers that would be impossible with traditional breeding. In particular, transgenics involves modifying cell information by artificially transferring genes from one species into another. This process is often called genetic engineering. It allows the insertion of genes from any plant, animal or bacteria into any other organism. Traditional breeding can only exchange genes between similar species. Examples of transgenics have included insect resistant potatoes, which have a bacterial gene added, and tomatoes whose storage qualities have been enhanced through the addition of a fish gene.

The potential benefits from transgenics are very large. Food supplies can be expanded to meet the needs of a rapidly growing global population. The technology can be used to heal the sick and to protect the healthy. It can ease problems of environmental pollution and help reclaim severely eroded land resources. It has the potential to create a whole new selection of renewable resources. However, the new technology also brings with it questions about the human health ramifications of long-term use and whether their release can negatively impact the environment. Typically, the proponents of biotechnology have focused on its potential benefits while its detractors have played up the potential risks. In truth, there is simply too little information to make more than an educated guess as to its full ramifications.

The potential value of trade that could be affected by transgenics is very large. At the moment, the United States is the global leader in approving transgenics for commercial production. The US lead in investment in R & D is much less pronounced, particularly relative to European-based transnational agribusiness firms. Currently, even in the United States, commercial production is confined to a handful of crops – peppers, carrots, potatoes, tomatoes, rapeseed, corn (maize), soybeans and milk. As transgenic products are not (as yet) segregated in production and distribution, all trade in these commodities will be affected. These crops represent approximately 35 per cent of US agricultural and food exports. If processed cereals and livestock that could have eaten transgenic feed are added, the total proportion of affected US exports rises to 70 per cent. Of course, these products also represent important ingredients in most processed foods further increasing the value of trade affected. Canada and Australia, too, have approved transgenic products for commercial production. In 1998, 35 million hectares were planted to transgenics worldwide, more than twice the 1997 area. In 1997, 3000 field trials were conducted, including 900 in the European Union. Research on literally thousands of products is reaching an advanced stage. In recent years US firms have registered 50 per cent of the world's patents in biotechnology, followed by EU firms with 33 per cent and Japanese firms with only 7 per cent.

The use of transgenics in prepared foods is widespread. For example, soy derivative products are used in approximately 60 per cent of processed foods. These include pasta, breakfast cereals, bread, ice cream, margarine, soya sauce and vegetarian meat substitutes. In general, the pace of change in all aspects of the technology is very rapid. The entire food system is in disequilibrium. Given the rapid rates of change, it is probably not surprising that consumers in places like the European Union, where trust in the food safety system is relatively low, are unsettled by the arrival of trangenics into their marketplace.

Those who are concerned about the introduction of transgenic products into their markets have three main concerns about the technology. The first relates to a philosophical unease with the underlying technology itself. These individuals perceive the technology to be 'unnatural' in the sense that it allows scientists to accomplish what nature will not allow in the normal course of events. They are also likely to worry about the ethical and moral ramifications of non-transgenic reproductive technologies, such as cloning. Transgenics is sometimes perceived as 'messing with God's work'. While these issues also create a degree of unease among the broader population, some individuals tend to hold very strong views on them. Transgenics appears to be a sufficiently radical technology to have induced many of those who hold strong views to become politically active.

The second concern with biotechnology relates to long-run food safety. No one seriously believes that eating a transgenic tomato for lunch will lead to violent illness by mid-afternoon. No such transgenic product would survive the current licensing system. The real concern is with consuming transgenic products over the long term. Could there be toxic build-ups in the body? Could the human immune system be weakened? Do we know enough about how these new genetic organisms react with human biology? These are the types of questions current food approval systems are ill designed to answer. Experiments with laboratory animals and other testing procedures are not perfect predictors of human experience. In some sense, the only way these questions can be completely answered is for consumption to take place over the long term – and, if consumption is not allowed to take place, then society will never know.

Those who believe that the benefits from the technology will be large often think that the existing scientific evidence suggests that the risks are sufficiently low for licensing to proceed. Those who see little benefit read the same evidence as supporting what they perceive as an extremely risky experiment. These two groups of protagonists, both with strong preferences, have been working hard to win over the minds and hearts of the public and politicians. There is, of course, a sizeable group of consumers who were already worried about the healthiness of their food – rejecting chemical residues in favour of organics, animal protein in favour of a vegetarian diet and so on and who see transgenics as simply the newest manifestation of the perversion of food consumption. It is probably unfortunate that the earliest transgenic foods produced commercially have largely agronomic benefits. As a result, farmers and agribusiness firms reap the benefit, but not consumers – except in the form of lower prices that are difficult to observe. Given that applications of transgenics have the potential to alter foods in ways that bring consumers considerable benefits – in terms of health and taste – early releases of these types of products might have altered the content of the debate.

The third concern about biotechnology relates to the release of transgenic organisms into the environment. As some of the transgenic products currently produced commercially have built in resistance to insects or chemicals, the question of whether those traits can be transferred to plants in the natural environment to create super-weeds has been raised. Will there be unforeseen externalities, such as genetic pest resistance threatening desirable insects as well as those it was designed to resist? Again, these types of questions tend to have definitive answers only in the long run. Those who are pro-biotechnology suggest that the existing scientific evidence points to a low level of risk of an environmental disaster. Those who worry about the environmental effects of transgenics use the same information to conclude that the risks are too high. Again, there is a sizeable group of individuals who were very concerned about the state of the environment before transgenics and for whom the new technology is simply a further step along the road to an unsustainable ecosystem.

There is one final group of individuals who have strongly held views about biotechnology, but their concern is not with the technology itself. Their concern is with the heavy involvement of transnational corporations in the development and commercialization of transgenic products. This group has had longstanding reservations about the role that they perceive large corporations have in shaping the economy. They see transgenics as a means for large corporations to strengthen their hold on food production – one of the central elements of human existence.

These four groups with strongly held preferences have found in transgenics an issue upon which they can agree. Individually, they have considerable skill at using the media to get their point across. They have been aided in some countries by the media itself which has found that a few well-turned phrases such as 'Frankenstein foods' garners considerable attention. In Europe, those with strongly held concerns about biotechnology have been able to outmanoeuvre the corporations and government officials who have ventured into the media fray.

The basic problem is that there is incomplete information regarding biotechnology and its ramifications. Political leaders around the world are scrambling to react to rising consumer concerns. The reaction in the European Union has been to move into a 'go slow' mode on approvals and research trials. Slowing down government approval, however, has trade effects because commercial production is already taking place in a number of countries that wish to export to the European Union.

4.5 INFORMATION ISSUES AND BIOTECHNOLOGY

Especially in Europe, biotechnology has become extremely contentious in spite of the fact that current scientific evidence often points to 'substantive equivalence' between genetically modified foods (GMFs) and their corresponding non-GMFs. As suggested in the previous section, public objections to transgenics can usually be categorized as: (1) long-term human health concerns; (2) long-term environmental concerns; and (3) ethical concerns. In many cases, the large multinational firms that are investing in biotechnology have themselves become a lightning rod for further public protest.

Biotechnology causes market failure or inefficiency for several reasons. To begin with, biotechnology markets are typically open entry oligopolies rather than competitive industries. Prices exceed marginal costs, leading to inefficiency of a type commonly associated with monopoly. While the costs involved in R & D constitute a barrier to entry, firms will continue to enter the market so long as they expect abnormally high profits. Thus, in a long-run equilibrium there will be a strong tendency for entry to dissipate super-normal profits.[1]

There are at least two additional reasons that biotechnology is likely to cause market failure, both probably more important from an international trade perspective.   First, biotechnology poses pervasive hidden quality problems. When consumers are apprehensive over possible, but as yet unknown, health problems that may arise from directly consuming GMFs, non-GMFs will be perceived as being of higher quality. However, consumers are often unable to costlessly identify non-GMFs and differentiate them from GMFs. A second source of market failure arises whenever there is a negative public-good aspect to GMF production and imports. Environmental and ethical concerns associated with biotechnology may imply that an individual is indirectly, and adversely, affected by both aggregate GMF production and GMF imports regardless of whether the GMF is consumed directly. In this section we focus first and foremost on the information issues associated with hidden quality but, subsequently, we will also consider the 'public-bad' problem.

In the previous section, we saw that eventually many GMFs may be designed with characteristics – such as health benefits or a longer shelf life – that are desirable for consumers. Such consumer-oriented genetic modifications will pose few informational issues since either they will be directly verifiable by consumers or their characteristics will be credibly revealed to consumers by producers. In this section we focus on the current wave of agronomic-oriented genetic modifications that have farm input-reducing and potentially cost-reducing features, such as products allowing reduced pesticide applications. Over the supply chain as a whole, information is asymmetric in these cases. Farmers, as well as the producers of biotechnology inputs themselves, have full information on whether particular crops are genetically modified.[2] In the absence of an effective identity preservation system (IPS) involving labelling and certification, however, the co-mingling of products causes information to become progressively more incomplete as the product moves downstream through the supply chain from farms to processors and on to distributors and retailers. Although farm-level producers are fully informed about the genetic qualities of their products, the final consumers will often be unable to determine whether a particular batch of a final product contains genetically modified material.[3] We assume highly stylized supply chains in which processors, distributors and retailers are perfectly competitive. For simplicity we also assume that each stage in the chain is initially costless and remains so unless labelling requirements force the separation of supply chains. Thus, in the absence of labelling, it is as if farm-level producers sell to final consumers.

In the absence of an IPS, the available information will sustain only a single blended market and a so-called 'pooling equilibrium'. Such hidden-type situations tend to generate 'adverse selection' whereby markets become dominated by an inefficient proportion of low-quality products, or what Akerlof (1970) calls 'lemons' (Plunkett and Gaisford, 2000).[4] The hidden-quality problem posed by the advent of a new GMF potentially could be addressed by an IPS (Hadfield and Thomson, 1998; Hobbs and Plunkett, 1999). A fully effective IPS would lead to separate markets for GMFs and non-GMFs and, thus, to a 'separating equilibrium'.

Perceptions of quality differences between GMFs and non-GMFs, of course, may vary significantly across countries. We follow Gaisford and Lau (2000) in considering an international trade situation where a new GMF is perceived as a lower-quality product in Europe but not elsewhere. For simplicity, we assume that Europe prohibits domestic production of the GMF. Given that Europe is an importer, its policy alternatives include: (1) allowing unlabelled GMF imports; (2) imposing an import embargo on the GMF; or (3) allowing labelled GMF imports. While the advent of the GMF may be welfare reducing regardless of which alternative is selected, an import embargo is virtually never the best policy.

The impact of allowing unlabelled GMF imports can be assessed using Figure 4.2. Europe's supply curve is S and its demand curve is Di prior to the introduction of the GMF. The initial pre-GMF world price is Pi. Consequently, European consumption is equal to DQi and European production is SQi with imports making up the difference. As a result of the development of a new biotechnology, the GMF imports become available at a price of Pf and non-GMF imports are no longer available. Consumer willingness to pay falls and the demand curve shifts downward to the pooled demand curve, Dp, as a result of the decline in average quality. Domestic output falls to SQp and domestic consumption settles at DQp. There are two opposing effects on European welfare. On the one hand, the decline in willingness to pay reduces consumer surplus by areas t, v and x at

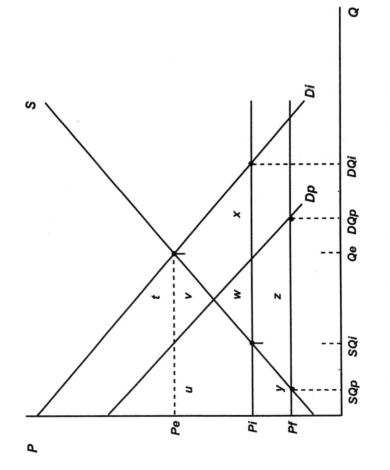

Figure 4.2: Unlabelled GMF imports versus an import embargo

the initial price of Pi. The loss of $t + v + x$ euros in Figure 4.2 thus represents an 'adverse quality effect' from the introduction of the GMF. On the other hand, the price reduction from Pi to Pf causes an increase in consumer surplus equal to areas $y + z$ and a decline in producer surplus of y euros. Thus, there is a 'beneficial price effect' of z euros. The overall impact on European welfare is therefore equal to $z - (t + v + x)$ euros. If the beneficial net price effect outweighed the adverse quality effect, Europe would gain from the new biotechnology, but in Figure 4.2 the adverse quality effect dominates (that is, areas $t + v + x$ exceed area z) and European welfare falls.

Now suppose that Europe imposes an import embargo instead of allowing unlabelled GMF imports. In this case, only non-GMFs remain available and the adverse quality effect does not arise. There is, however, a harmful price effect. The relevant demand curve remains Di in Figure 4.2. Since non-GMF imports are unavailable, the quantity produced and consumed in Europe is Qe and the price rises to Pe. Producer surplus rises by $u + v$ euros, but consumer surplus falls by $u + v + w + x$ euros. Thus European welfare unambiguously declines because of an 'adverse price effect' of $w + x$ euros. Europe may, however, lose less by prohibiting imports than by allowing unlabelled GMF imports. Recall that the change in welfare with unlabelled access is $z - (t + v + x)$ euros and the change in welfare with the embargo is $- (w + x)$ euros. The embargo is superior, therefore, if area $t + v$ exceeds area $w + z$, which happens to be the case in Figure 4.2. Of course, in other cases the embargo will be worse.

The third policy alternative is a mandatory IPS requiring the labelling of GMF imports. With such an IPS, there will be separate markets for the non-GMF product (good 1) and the GMF product (good 2). Initially the GMF is not available, so only market 1 is relevant in Figure 4.3. The initial European demand curve for the non-GMF is $D1i$ (which corresponds to Di in Figure 4.2), the European supply curve is $S1$ (which corresponds to S) and the initial world price is $P1i$ (which corresponds to Pi). Initial domestic consumption is $DQ1i$ (which is equal to DQi in Figure 4.2) and initial domestic production is $SQ1i$ (which is equal to SQi). Notice, once again, that if an embargo were imposed to block the import of the new GMF, the equilibrium quantity would be $Q1e$ (which equals Qe in Figure 4.2) and the equilibrium price would be $P1e$ (which equals Pe). The European welfare loss from employing the embargo response is $c + e + f$ euros (which equals $w + x$ euros in Figure 4.2).

Mandatory labelling of GMF imports gives rise to a separating equilibrium. European consumers can choose to buy the high-quality non-GMF in market 1, which continues to be supplied by domestic producers. Alternatively, they can buy the low-quality GMF in market 2, which is supplied by offshore producers. The GMF price, $P2s$, exceeds the price at which the GMF can be imported (that is, Pf in Figure 4.2) due to labelling and sorting costs. The advent of the GMF, which gives rise to market 2, shifts the demand curve for the non-GMF to $D1s$ in market 1. The new substitute product, albeit of lower perceived quality, takes some demand away from the old product. In Figure 4.3 we take $D1s$ to be the demand for the non-GMF when the price of the GMF is $P2s$ while $D2s$ is the demand curve for the GMF when the price of the non-GMF is $P1s$. In the separating equilibrium, $Q1s$ units of the non-GMF are purchased at the price of $P1s$, and $Q2s$ units of the GMF are bought at the price of $P2s$. Due to the perceived quality difference, $P1s$ necessarily exceeds $P2s$. Notice, however, that $P1s$ could be less than $P1i$ if the inward shift in the $D1$ demand curve was sufficiently large.

We assess the impact of mandatory labelling of GMF imports on European markets by considering the two markets in sequence. Prior to the introduction of the GMF, its price is effectively infinite and the demand for non-GMF is $D1i$. We start in the non-GMF market and raise the price from $P1i$ to $P1s$ while holding the price of the GMF at its initial infinite level. Since the relevant curve remains $D1i$, the change in consumer surplus is a loss of $d + e + f$ euros. The gain in producer surplus is d euros, so that there is an overall adverse 'price effect' of $e + f$ euros on high-quality market 1. With the price of the non-GMF already changed to $P1s$, we turn to the GMF market where the relevant demand curve is $D2s$. Here there is a gain in new consumer surplus of g euros, which is a 'beneficial new-product effect'. The overall effect on Europe of allowing GMF imports with mandatory labelling is equal to $g - (e + f)$ euros. It should be emphasized that whenever the beneficial new-product effect outweighs the harmful price effect on the old product, European welfare rises. In Figure 4.3, however, the adverse price effect dominates and European welfare falls in spite of labelling.

Figure 4.3 can also be used to compare an import embargo with a mandatory labelling policy. Whereas $e + f$ euros are lost in the non-GMF market with mandatory labelling, $c + e + f$ euros are lost with the embargo. The harmful price effect on market 1 is smaller with mandatory labelling

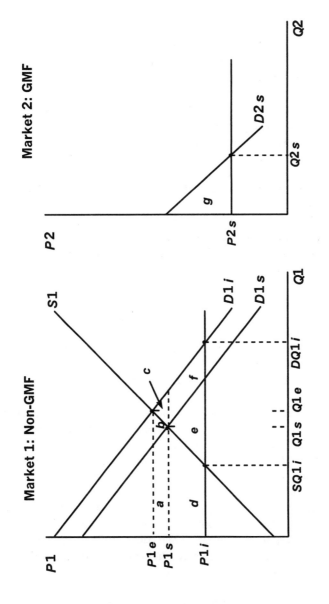

Figure 4.3: Labelled GM imports versus an import embargo

because the price of the non-GMF generally rises less under mandatory labelling than under the import embargo. The demand curve for the non-GMF shifts to the left as a result of the presence of the low-quality GMF substitute product and mitigates or even reverses the upward pressure on $P1$.[5] Further, in the non-GMF market there is a gain of g euros from mandatory labelling that does not arise with the embargo. Thus the mandatory labelling of GMF imports is unambiguously better than an import embargo by $c + g$ euros.

While a policy of mandatory labelling of GMF imports typically dominates an import embargo, labelling need not always be better than no labelling. The costs of labelling GMFs may be significant if there is a need to prevent adulteration of GMFs with non-GMFs because supply chains would have to be kept separate to prevent the co-mingling of products. On the one hand, if the perceived quality differences are sufficiently small, the labelling and sorting costs of moving to a separating or two-market situation, rather than a pooling or one-market situation, will exceed the benefits and labelling should not be required. On the other hand, when the perceived quality difference is large, GMF labelling should be obligatory. In no cases, however, are import embargoes warranted.

To this point, we have focused on GMFs as exclusively private goods, but GMFs pose some additional public-goods issues. For example, some Europeans may be concerned about aggregate GMF production, consumption and import levels on environmental and animal health grounds as well as on human health and ethical grounds. Since the aggregate quantities for GMFs are likely to be observable, externalities or non-market effects rather than hidden quality issues are central. The social costs of GMF production, consumption and imports may well exceed the private costs. In the absence of corrective policy, the overproduction, overconsumption and overimportation of GMFs would be expected.

In the presence of negative GMF externalities, prohibitions on production and/or imports may sometimes improve welfare in comparison with *laissez faire* or non-intervention. While occasionally such policies may be optimal, this is not generally the case. Rather, so-called Pigouvian taxes on production and imports would be warranted. Such taxes are set to cover external costs and bring marginal social costs, rather than private costs, into line with marginal benefits. Suppose that only long-term, as yet unknown environmental consequences of a new biotechnology are feared by Europeans. For instance, the release of a genetically modified organism

(GMO) into the environment may be a potential threat to indigenous species. Further, take the extreme case where these biodiversity fears warrant a prohibitive tax on domestic agricultural use of the new biotechnology in Europe. Even in this case, a prohibitive import tax on the GMF import may not be efficient. Whereas imports may pose a greater risk of inadvertent or opportunistic release of GMOs into the European environment, this compares with the certainty of release with European agricultural production. While there is a valid argument for permitting corrective taxes on GMF imports, a blanket case for import embargoes cannot be sustained. Even the case for taxation of GMF imports depends on the degree of offshore processing, since products with no reproductive potential should not be subject to tax on biodiversity grounds. Clearly biotechnology poses multiple challenges for rule-making in international trade. We now turn to the exploration of those challenges.

4.6 BIOTECHNOLOGY AND THE WTO

The three WTO agreements pertaining to biotechnology – the SPS, the TBT and the TRIPS – are not part of the URAA. However, the problems that biotechnology has the potential to create for the institutions of international trade suggest that there may be considerable pressure to open those agreements for further negotiation.

The TRIPS is the simplest to deal with, but even with it there are complex issues. Biotechnology is an industry founded on intellectual property. The expected returns from the investments being made in biotechnology are expected to come from the ability to capture a considerable portion of the value created by intellectual endeavours. For this to be accomplished there needs to be strong protection· of intellectual property rights. This generally exists in developed market economies. It has not been the case in developing economies, and the TRIPS was insisted upon by developed countries at the Uruguay Round so that the threat of trade actions could be used to induce stronger protection for intellectual property rights in developing countries.

The companies investing in biotechnology require strong intellectual property protection because the lifecycle of their products is likely to be extremely short. The pace of technological improvement is likely to be very rapid and the window for recouping investments narrow. This means that firms investing in biotechnology need access to the widest possible markets for their products. Markets are only truly accessible if intellectual property rights are protected. The TRIPS enforcement mechanisms, while as yet untested, appear to be weak (see Section 4.3).

Firms developing biotechnology may lobby their governments to have the TRIPS re-opened in the hope of strengthening it. Acceptance of the desirability of strengthening intellectual property protection was lukewarm at best in developing countries at the Uruguay Round. Two of the areas where concerns were the greatest were agricultural inputs and pharmaceuticals. The fear was that protecting intellectual property in these areas would raise the cost of drugs and food for low-income populations. Of course, agricultural inputs and pharmaceuticals are the two main focuses of current research in biotechnology. Developing countries, having been forced to accede to the TRIPS at the Uruguay Round, may resist its re-opening. Given that little R & D in biotechnology goes on in developing countries, they perceive that they have little to gain.

Some developing countries, however, have begun to worry about what they perceive as the plundering of their rich stock of genetic material by biotechnology companies in search of potentially profitable genes (Kerr, Hobbs and Yampoin, 1999). The TRIPS currently exempts non-genetically engineered plants from protection. The concerns over 'biopiracy' may be sufficient inducement for developed countries to allow the TRIPS to be opened and a mutually beneficial compromise reached.

The SPS and TBT will be the main focus of the trade issues surrounding biotechnology. The international conventions pertaining to health, sanitary and phyto-sanitary-based barriers to trade are premised on the principle that the 'best available scientific information' will be used to justify their establishment and in their regulatory design. There are two aspects to this principle – 'appropriate science', and risk assessment (Caswell and Hooker, 1996).

While scientists may disagree on specifics, there is probably a near-consensus among the scientific community regarding what constitutes 'appropriate science'. It concerns the application of the scientific method, and involves the drawing up of hypotheses based on existing scientific knowledge, devising and conducting tests of those hypotheses and establishing protocols for the ongoing monitoring of processes in a commercial environment. The rationale for tying import regulations and hence domestic requirements to an 'appropriate science' criterion in the SPS is to prevent the capricious use of health, sanitary and phyto-sanitary regulations as a non-tariff barrier.

There is, however, a further implicit assumption underpinning the 'appropriate science' criterion. It is that consumers will accept, or defer to, the judgement of the scientific community regarding what constitutes 'appropriate science'. In the case of biotechnology there appears to be a considerable segment of society that is no longer willing to accept passively the scientific evidence used by those scientists charged with ensuring human, animal and plant health and environmental protection. Without consumer agreement on what would constitute 'appropriate science', it has become almost impossible to make trade policy for GMFs that is consistent with existing WTO commitments.

Consumer concerns will mean that the approval of transgenics may be delayed or denied. As a result, countries will wish to use trade barriers to keep transgenic products out of their markets. This will lead to disputes at the WTO.

The SPS states that sanitary and phyto-sanitary measures are to be applied only to the extent necessary to protect human, animal or plant life and health. They are to be based on scientific principles and not to be maintained without scientific evidence. Given the paucity of scientific evidence to suggest that transgenics is harmful, it will be difficult for countries to defend their import restrictions at the WTO.

Restrictions on trade are also supposed to be made on the basis of a risk assessment. Risk, however, is premised on sufficient data being available to calculate probabilities. Currently, there is insufficient information on the long-term effects of transgenics to objectively establish the degree of risk involved and hence the problem is one of uncertainty. Politicians are responding to uncertainty and so will not be able to provide credible risk assessments to be scrutinized by their trade partners.

It would seem that the 'appropriate science' and risk assessment criteria enshrined in the SPS were not designed to deal with the types of problems presented by the introduction of transgenics. The current situation regarding transgenic products is a disequilibrium. The type of situation that the SPS was designed to deal with was an equilibrium situation. Its mechanisms appear to envisage a situation where the science involved is not controversial. Further, the SPS assumes that the product will have been around for sufficient time for risk assessments to be made on the basis of well-understood parameters. In this equilibrium situation, if a country attempted to put a trade restriction in place justified on health, sanitary or phyto-sanitary reasons, but it was actually a premeditated non-tariff barrier, the country whose market access was denied would be able to appeal to a

WTO disputes panel. The panel could compare the scientific justification put forward by the imposing country against the accepted scientific standard. The risk assessment could also be examined to see if it was consistent with other risk assessments in the country wishing to impose the trade barrier. This scenario closely parallels what transpired in the dispute over EU restrictions on the importation of beef produced using hormones (Roberts, 1998). The hormone case suggests that the SPS is working as intended to prevent the capricious use of trade restrictions justified on sanitary and phyto-sanitary grounds.

The SPS clearly permits trade measures to be put in place when a government considers the existing scientific evidence insufficient to permit a final decision on the safety of a product (Stanton, 1995). A country invoking this clause must be actively seeking the information required. The 'insufficient information' justification for the imposition of trade barriers was clearly meant as a temporary measure. Thus it would seem that countries could invoke this justification for imposing trade barriers against transgenic products. Such a justification, however, would certainly be challenged at the WTO.

There would seem to be two ways a WTO panel could proceed in the case of a complaint against trade barriers being imposed on the basis of insufficient information. First, it could put the onus on the complaining party to prove that sufficient information does exist to evaluate the particular transgenic product excluded. This shifting of the burden of proof away from the defending country might be a precedent member countries would wish to avoid in the wider context of the WTO. The second option would be for the disputes panel to refuse to hear the case because no objective determination could be made. Taking this course might, however, lead to countries being able to resort to this justification in a wide range of disputes. The European Union has suggested that the 'precautionary principle' be used for cases of uncertainty. However, the 'precautionary principle' is not sufficiently developed as a decision-making rule to prevent its being used capriciously to provide protection (Phillips and Kerr, 2000). The United States and other exporting countries can be expected to resist vigorously the inclusion of the 'precautionary principle' in the WTO.

A refusal to hear a case would only reduce the credibility of the WTO and lead countries to seek other means to settle their disputes over GMFs. The major problem, of course, is that the SPS is not designed to handle cases where consumers are demanding protection, particularly when consumers have little faith in the scientific community. There needs to be a forum where government responses to consumers demands for protection can be dealt with directly (Perdikis and Kerr, 1999).

As discussed in the previous section, an alternative to banning GMFs from the market would be for countries to introduce strict labelling of imports containing genetically modified organisms. This would mean that governments would remove themselves from having to make a determination on the safety of GMFs and instead would be allowing consumers to decide whether they are willing to consume the product or not. This type of regulation would come under the TBT. The problem is that labelling could impose considerable costs on firms attempting to market transgenic-free products. Presumably the reason for labelling products in the first place would be to provide consumers with a choice. Unless there is a reason to keep GMFs strictly untainted by non-GMFs, gaining market access through labelling is a simple task for firms selling transgenic products. Label it and sell it. No one will question the label because consumers are unlikely to care if their product contains non-transgenic products even if it is labelled as containing transgenic products. On the other hand, consumers would be disturbed if what they considered to be transgenic-free products actually contained transgenic material. This means that those selling transgenic-free products will have to ensure the credibility of their labels. This will require the introduction of identity preservation systems, which may be expensive relative to the benefits received by consumers and lead to disputes based on the TBT criteria discussed in Section 4.2.

It seems clear that biotechnology will be a very contentious issue in agricultural trade. As a result, it is likely to be the subject of many disputes and lead to calls for the re-negotiation of a number of WTO agreements.

4.7 ANTI-DUMPING AND COUNTERVAIL

4.7.1 Contingent Protection

Anti-dumping and countervail are two trade actions that come under the general category of contingent protection. They deal with issues concerning 'fair trade'. Countries are allowed to put contingent trade measures in place when firms in their markets are faced with competition from foreign sources that are trading 'unfairly'. The trade measures applied are normally tariffs but the WTO does allow other measures such as import quotas in certain circumstances. The trade measures are put in place to offset the injury suffered. They are contingent measures in the sense that they will only remain in place until the unfair practice ceases – that is, they are contingent upon the removal of the offending activity. While contingent protection measures have been around since the beginning of the 20th century, they were seldom used until recent years.

The use of contingent protection measures has increased considerably as trade barriers have come down as a result of the general GATT success in liberalizing trade. The offences of dumping and countervailable subsidies are poorly defined at the WTO and actions are often brought even when trade is not being undertaken under circumstances that economic theory would suggest should be of concern. There is a general perception that contingent protection measures are open to abuse and can be used to harass foreign firms. In short, they have become the new weapon of protectionists. While all of this is well understood, there is little political will to change it. Contingent protection is popular with some policy makers because it is a cheap way to divert protectionist energies away from direct lobbying of politicians for protection.

Agriculture is particularly vulnerable to contingent protection measures. As a result, agricultural exporters have a special interest in seeing the system either abolished or improved. Of course, agricultural protectionists have been major beneficiaries of the existing provisions, primarily as a result of it being effective in harassing foreign competitors. Members of the US Congress are particularly fond of contingent protection measures and are unlikely to want them opened up for further negotiation. The issue is sufficiently emotive, however, that re-negotiation cannot be put off forever. There was a strong push to have contingent protection put on the agenda for a new round of negotiations at the Seattle WTO Ministerial Meeting in November 1999.

4.7.2 Anti-dumping

The anti-dumping provisions in the WTO are unique in that they are directed at the activities of private firms rather than governments. The underlying economic rationale of anti-dumping is one of the most muddled in the WTO. The absence of a solid economic underpinning leads to most of the abuse of the anti-dumping code and must be addressed if it is to be less open to abuse. The WTO anti-dumping code is not helpful on this point as it simply provides a definition of dumping without any explanation of the unfair business practice it is intended to redress (Tharakan, 1999). This absence of rationale is telling in itself and suggests either confusion or disagreement among the contracting parties to the WTO.

Instead of going to the definition of dumping provided in the GATT code, which only serves to cloud the issue, we will attempt what the WTO contracting parties have failed (or refused) to do – develop a reasonable economic argument as to what practice anti-dumping ought to redress. What practice of private business is considered 'unfair' in domestic competition policy legislation? The one that seems to correspond most closely to the muddle at the WTO is 'predatory pricing'. Predatory pricing is the purposeful selling below cost in a market to drive out the competition so that the market can be monopolized.[6] Predatory pricing is accomplished by cross-subsidizing the losses in the market being preyed upon with profits made in other markets. This implies different prices in two markets that can be kept separate to prevent arbitrage. Predatory pricing could certainly take place internationally and domestic competition policy could not provide a remedy against a foreign predator. Anti-dumping duties applied at a rate equal to the difference between the prices would seem a reasonable, if crude, proxy to eliminate the threat of predation. It should be noted that predatory pricing is not compatible with short-run profit maximization because the predatory firm is selling below cost in one market, accepting losses in the short run with the incentive of reaping monopoly profits in the long run.

Predatory pricing is an old concept in economics. It is used to explain how markets can be monopolized. While it is a possible method by which to monopolize a market, it is a relatively costly one. McGee (1958) makes a compelling argument that it is much more profitable for firms wishing to monopolize a market to do so by purchasing or merging with competitors. The argument is sufficiently strong to suggest that international predatory pricing would be sufficiently rare that the entire anti-dumping edifice could be done away with. One possible reason for foreign firms to engage in predatory pricing would be if foreign investment were prohibited or otherwise controlled. However, casual examination of recent anti-dumping actions does not seem to verify this hypothesis. In any case, anti-dumping is still part of international trade law.

There are two stylized facts associated with international predatory pricing. The first is a lower price in the importing (predated) market than in the exporter's home market. The second is that the product is sold below cost in the predated market. These two stylized facts, even when taken together, are not sufficient to prove that predatory pricing is taking place. It is easy to demonstrate that any firm with the ability to price-discriminate will charge different prices in different markets in the course of profit maximization. As the average total cost of production depends upon both fixed and variable costs, it is also easy to show that in the short run a profit-maximizing price-discriminating firm could be making a profit in both markets, making a loss in both markets, or selling at a profit in the high-priced market and at a loss in the low-priced market. The latter is not predatory pricing because it represents short-run profit maximization and there is no attempt to drive out competition.

If one takes the two stylized facts separately, neither is evidence of unfair business practice. Selling at different prices in different markets is evidence of market power but not of unfair trade being practised against domestic firms. After all, if the firm is making a profit then removing its market power would lower the price of the product, which was not the result intended when anti-dumping duties were contemplated. If the firm is losing money consistently then it will exit the market and there is no need to worry about the charging of two prices.

Selling below cost taken alone is not evidence of unfair business practice. It is not considered unfair domestically unless it is predatory pricing. Firms often sell below cost – lose money – in the short run either because markets are depressed or because they have unforeseen inventories. Having discount sales is perceived as normal business practice and beneficial to consumers. If the products discounted for sale originate in a foreign country, it is still not an unfair business practice. While all of these stylized facts individually or taken together may be evidence of predatory pricing, they are not sufficient in themselves to prove that it is taking place. Given this background, how is dumping defined at the WTO?

According to Article 2.1 of the WTO Anti-dumping Agreement:

> a product is considered as being dumped, i.e. introduced into the commerce of another country at less than its normal value, if the export price of the product exported from one country to another is less than the comparable price, in the ordinary course of trade, for the like product when destined for consumption in the exporting country.

This is the definition upon which WTO members have based their domestic legislation. No wonder there are problems in implementation.

Price discrimination, if nothing else is considered, is dumping. As suggested above, there is no economic justification for price discrimination alone to be considered an unfair business practice in terms of domestic producers competing with imported products.

Under certain circumstances, the WTO Anti-dumping Agreement allows the use of a constructed price as an alternative to – but not in conjunction with – the price discrimination definition. According to Article 2.2.1:

> sales at prices below per unit (fixed and variable) costs of production plus administrative and general costs may be treated as not being in the ordinary course of trade, if the authorities determine that the sales were made within a substantial period of time and in substantial quantities.

One should note that this is a constructed cost based on average total cost. Second, note that there is no precise definition of the term 'substantial period'.

Agriculture is particularly vulnerable to the use of this definition in isolation, for three reasons. In agricultural production there is often a considerable lag between the decision to commit resources to production and the time when harvesting/slaughter takes place. Due to the vagaries of weather and pests, poor yields may mean that costs cannot be covered at harvest. In addition, as harvesting must often take place within a short period if quality is to be maintained, harvesting decisions are often based, not on the total production cost, but rather on whether harvesting cost alone will be covered by expected price (Schmitz Firch and Hillman, 1981). Finally, many animal industries suffer from cycles that are in part biologically based, and farmers typically sell below cost for extended periods at the bottom of a cycle. This is normal business practice. Given the elastic definition of a 'substantial period', crop years, harvesting seasons and cyclical troughs can all be covered. It is ironic that, in well-integrated markets such as those of the NAFTA, farmers on both sides of the border can be at the bottom of the same price cycle and losing money, yet farmers on one side of the border who are exporting can be the subject of an anti-dumping action.

Given the problems with the definition of dumping, Tharakan (1999) suggests that 'the anti-dumping system is now poised to become the most important trade-restricting device in the post-Uruguay Round world' (p. 180). While there is considerable political resistance to opening up anti-dumping for re-negotiation, the theoretical inconsistencies and potential for abuse suggest that 'sooner or later this debate is likely to be resumed at the WTO' (Koulen, 1995, p. 232). The special circumstances of agriculture need to be addressed if the Agreement is re-opened.

4.7.3 Countervail

Countervailing duties are applied when 'unfair' subsidization is deemed to be taking place. In the general WTO system, this happens when injury is proven and either a country refuses to cease the use of prohibited subsidies or actionable subsidies are being used at levels above the *de minimis* levels. The reclassification of subsidies into categories (boxes) reduced much of the ambiguity that existed in the pre-Uruguay Round GATT. The exemptions granted agricultural subsidies also reduced the use of countervail and the threat of countervail in agriculture.

The major problem with countervail, which also applies to dumping to some extent, relates to the determination of injury and the calculation of the size of the duty to apply. The problem of injury determination relates to the economic concept of *ceterus paribus*. To prove injury it should be necessary to demonstrate that, subject to all other things being constant, the unfair subsidy was the cause of injury. Of course, many forces affect markets, so isolating the effects of one is a complex problem. The measures used by countries to determine injury, however, are inconsistent and often not theoretically defensible. As a result, they are open to manipulation or biased in favour of finding injury. The problems pertaining to determining the size of the penalty to be applied are similar and relate to the averaging of subsidies and inconsistencies among methodologies. Common criteria need to be developed. These criteria need to be theoretically sound.

4.7.4 The Future of Contingent Protection

Contingent protection has become an important issue at the WTO. This may be because of the absence of the political will to reform it – even in the face of widespread criticism, obvious theoretical deficiencies and blatant abuse of its mechanisms. It has become one of the major weapons in the protectionist arsenal. The WTO will not be fully effective until significant improvements take place in the area of contingent protection. In part, improvement will have to wait for better economic analysis to underpin the trade rules. In the case of dumping, it has been suggested that attempting to harmonize competition policy may be a more fruitful avenue for reform. Until that happens, dumping is likely to remain firmly entrenched in international trade law.

4.8 REGIONAL TRADE ASSOCIATIONS AND THEIR ROLE IN AGRICULTURAL TRADE

Trade blocs or regional trade associations (RTAs), which consist of two or more countries usually in close geographic proximity, proliferated and became an increasingly important force in world trade during the 1980s and 1990s. It is usual to classify RTAs according to the degree of economic integration. The loosest type of RTA is a *free trade area*, where each country removes the internal trade barriers facing other member countries but retains an independent trade policy *vis-à-vis* non-members. Both the North American Free Trade Agreement (NAFTA) between the United States, Mexico and Canada, and the Australia New Zealand Closer Economic Relations Trade Agreement (ANZERT) are examples of free trade areas. Free trade areas require detailed rules of origin to prevent 'tariff circumvention' whereby non-member countries send their product to a high-tariff member via a low-tariff member.[7] NAFTA's general rules of origin stipulate that a good must be sufficiently different that its tariff classification is changed in one NAFTA country before it qualifies for tariff-free access to another NAFTA country. In addition, NAFTA applies much more stringent rules of origin to automobiles and to textiles and clothing.

The tariff circumvention problem can also be avoided through closer integration. In a *customs union*, such as MERCOSUR in South America, the countries not only remove internal barriers but also adopt a common external trade policy.[8] In a common market, integration proceeds further by allowing labour and capital mobility between member countries.

Finally, in an *economic union*, there is again regulatory harmonization and coordination of socio-economic policy. For example, an economic union may include a common currency. The European Union can now be classified as an economic union, but at its inception as the European Economic Community it was a common market.[9] Countries with a federal structure, such as the United States and Canada, can also be viewed as economic unions.

While this classification system is useful, many RTAs do not fit perfectly into any category. For example, NAFTA includes foreign investment or capital mobility provisions while Australia and New Zealand have agreed to use competition policy rather than anti-dumping duties on each other's firms under ANZERT.

The essence of any trade bloc or RTA is to provide preferential treatment for members. RTAs are in fact sometimes called preferential trading arrangements. Of course, this implies discrimination against non-members. While such preferences conflict with the usual GATT and WTO principle of non-discrimination, Article XXIV of the GATT and Article V of the General Agreement on Trade in Services (GATS) explicitly permit the formation of RTAs under certain circumstances. Officially, RTAs must provide full liberalization of essentially all trade between members. Unofficially, however, we will see that powerful countries and blocs have interpreted this requirement loosely and often leave out a broad range of sensitive agricultural products or even the entire agricultural sector. The WTO also requires predetermined, finite adjustment periods when RTAs are formed. In practice, this has meant that most of the internal barriers that are subject to reduction are eliminated within ten years. Finally, the WTO stipulates that external barriers should not rise. This requirement poses potential problems for any country joining an RTA that has a common external trade policy, such as the European Union. Where a new member has to raise its tariffs to harmonize with the RTA, it may be required to compensate outside trade partners or face retaliation. In Chapter 3, it was suggested that some central European countries are likely to face this issue as they accede to the European Union. Further, it was argued that, given the choice between paying compensation and accepting retaliation, the latter is generally the lesser of the two costs.

The formation of an RTA may or may not be jointly beneficial for the member countries. In addition to *trade creation*, the discriminatory nature of trade liberalization gives rise to the possibility of *trade diversion*. Suppose that Country 1 and Country 2 form an RTA, and consider a specific market where initially Country 1 happens to be an importer and Country 2 is an exporter. Further, assume for the moment that the world price remains unchanged and that the RTA is a free trade area. Pure trade creation occurs in this market if Country 2 is a sufficiently low-cost supplier that it can meet the full import demand of Country 1 at the world price. In this case, the domestic price in Country 1 will fall to the world price and create gains to consumers that more than offset the loss to producers and the loss of tariff revenue collected by the government. Since

Country 2 continues to ship some exports to the rest of the world, its price remains equal to the world price and its welfare is unaffected.

Pure trade diversion occurs when Country 2 is a sufficiently high-cost producer that it cannot meet Country 1's full import demand at Country 1's tariff-inclusive initial domestic price. In this case, Country 1 will continue to import some product from countries in the rest of the world under tariffs, but will also divert some imports to Country 2. In Country 2, the price will rise to Country 1's initial tariff-inclusive price because of the preferential or tariff-free access it gets to Country 1's market. In Country 2, producers gain more than consumers lose, but the resultant net gains to Country 2 are insufficient to compensate Country 1 for its loss of tariff revenue. Thus, considered jointly, the two countries would lose from the formation of an RTA in the case of this particular market.[10]

If world prices remain constant, the countries forming an RTA would experience joint gains in markets where pure trade creation occurs and joint losses in markets where pure trade diversion arises. Intermediate situations with elements of both trade creation and trade diversion can also occur when the price in the importing country falls part but not all of the way to the world price.[11] In situations where the integration proceeds beyond a free trade area, there are additional budgetary and tariff-harmonization effects that arise from adopting a common external trade policy. Further, common markets and economic unions open the possibility of gains and losses associated with increased internal factor mobility.

The formation of any type of RTA may lead to induced changes in world prices. Such world price changes have a tendency to be jointly beneficial to insider countries and harmful to outsiders. For example, in the case of pure trade diversion, Country 1 reduces its imports from outside countries, placing downward pressure on the world price. Since the two partners jointly are net importers, such a reduction in the world price is jointly beneficial to the partners. The countries in the rest of the world, however, will be worse off on average because jointly they are net exporters. Two additional empirically important sources of gains from RTAs should be mentioned. First, whenever RTAs promote more rapid economic growth, there will be dynamic trade creation gains that tend to be beneficial to insider and outsider countries alike. Second, by enlarging markets, RTAs promote further exploitation of economies of scale in imperfectly competitive industries and generate gains from intra-industry trade creation.

Agricultural trade has frequently posed profound problems for the formation of RTAs. Two broad approaches to agricultural trade can be identified. The first approach, which was adopted by the European Economic Community, is to include agricultural trade on a comprehensive basis. Due to the sensitivity of the agricultural sector, the Common Agricultural Policy (CAP) was developed as a broad support programme in tandem with the internal liberalization of agricultural trade so as to ensure the survival of most farmers in all member countries. The problems that have arisen with the CAP, as well as intrinsic difficulties, have made the comprehensive approach to agricultural trade in RTAs increasingly rare.

The alternative approach, which was adopted in most of the RTAs formed in the 1980s and 1990s, is to selectively liberalize agricultural trade. In this piecemeal approach, some commodities are partially or totally exempt from liberalization. For example, NAFTA has separate agreements on agricultural trade between Mexico and the United States and between Mexico and Canada, while agricultural trade between Canada and the United States is governed by the earlier Canada–US Free Trade Agreement. To protect Canada's systems of supply-limiting (managing) marketing boards, Canada–US and Canada–Mexico trade in the poultry and dairy sectors remain restricted.[12] Even in sectors where RTAs officially liberalize trade, controversies and disputes have often arisen. For example, Canada and the United States have had several disputes over hogs and beef where free trade is permitted. The issue of Canadian exports of durum wheat to the United States is particularly interesting because there is evidence that US export-enhancing policies led to higher US prices, which in turn attracted imports from Canada and protest by the United States.

The European Union, in its trade dealings with non-EU countries, has taken the selective approach to agricultural trade liberalization to an extreme. Free trade in manufactures, but not agricultural products, prevails in European Economic Area consisting of the European Union, Norway, Liechtenstein and Iceland. Similarly, agricultural trade is largely excluded from the European Union's Europe Agreements or Association Agreements with Mediterranean and central European countries.[13] The total or even partial exclusion of agricultural trade is highly questionable in view of the requirement in GATT Article XXIV that RTA members fully liberalize virtually all internal trade. Nevertheless, powerful trade entities such as the United States and the European Union have set the precedent whereby Article XXIV is interpreted very loosely. As long as the current WTO negotiations remain narrowly focused on the agenda that was pre-set by the Uruguay Round, Article XXIV will remain largely toothless. Nevertheless, in future WTO negotiations, it would be useful to clarify and preferably limit the ability of RTAs to exclude agricultural products from full trade liberalization.

4.9 ACCESSION OF CHINA AND RUSSIA TO THE WTO

While the accession of China, Russia and the other states of the former Soviet empire and sphere of influence that remain outside the WTO will not be a direct part of the negotiations which began in 2000, it will be in the background and will influence the negotiations in other areas. At least for some countries, accession negotiations are likely to be going on concurrently.

The reasons why the accession negotiations are important for agricultural trade are obvious. China and Russia have large populations. As incomes rise, they will increasingly be consumers of higher-quality and varied foodstuffs. They represent large potential markets. On the other hand, they also contribute significantly to global production. While China may not be a large net food exporter in the near future, and more likely a net importer, given the huge size of its economy, it has the potential to be a major export player in selective international markets. Russia is currently producing at levels far below its agronomic potential. Other New Independent States (NIS) of the former Soviet Union, such as the Ukraine, are also producing at levels that do not reflect their potential. If economic growth continues in China and economic reforms take hold in Russia, then their accession to the WTO will have a major impact on international markets for agricultural products.

Countries that are outside the WTO are not subject to the same trade rules as members. At best, a comprehensive set of rules can be negotiated bilaterally between two countries. What is more likely is that bilateral agreements are incomplete or do not exist at all. This means that trade relations are open to the most capricious actions of trade partners and are based on relative power. Anti-dumping and countervail can be applied without any international constraints. Tariffs need not be bound, import quotas can proliferate, and trade concessions can be withdrawn for political reasons.

Countries may also feel that it is advantageous to have trading partners outside the international system and its constraints. Export subsidies can be used to dispose of surpluses that can no longer be shipped to WTO members. The managers of the European Union's CAP have always found it useful to have access to the Russian market to dispose of surplus agricultural output. Once countries accede to the WTO, these convenient markets will no longer be available.

Once Russia and the other NIS countries join the WTO, it will be much more difficult for the neighbouring central European states to manage their eastern borders. The NIS and Russian agricultural markets are very volatile. Opening up to this degree of volatility may make the transition process in central Europe much more difficult.

China and Russia will represent a significant challenge for the WTO, yet excluding them makes a mockery of the organization's global ambitions. Russia and China do not represent a challenge simply because of their size and potential but also because the long period of command economy that both experienced has left their economies far short of a market economy. Both China and Russia have abandoned central planning as the heart of their economic system but this does not mean that they have fully embraced the market system (Kerr and MacKay, 1997).

The WTO is a system of rules for market economies. It is poorly designed to deal with other economic systems. In the past, some command economies did join the WTO; they were allowed to join largely for political reasons. It was never a happy marriage but the trading activities of these command economy members of the WTO were sufficiently small that their inherent incompatibilities could be ignored. This will not be the case with China or Russia. Their economies are simply too large to ignore.

China's official economic policy is a transition to 'market socialism'. While this term has an elastic and evolving definition, it seems unlikely that significant intervention to directly determine or indirectly affect prices will cease in the near future. As long as the Communist Party remains firmly in control, it will be interventionist (Ceko and Kerr, 2000). Prices established by fiat represent a significant problem for the WTO. Trade flows are supposed to represent underlying market values. Changes in trading patterns are expected to arise from changing relative efficiencies. If steel prices in China are set arbitrarily low and exports of steel-using products increase, what is the cause of the changing advantage? Trading partners are likely to cry foul. In a similar fashion, if the price of rice is depressed as a subsidy to consumers, exporting rice to China will be unattractive. Potential exporters will complain they have not been given market access. Further, the power to set prices can be used to strategically distort trade, just like border measures and subsidies. While single cases of price distortion can be netted out, when intervention in markets is endemic, prices in one market are costs to another and distortions multiply.

The Chinese economy is also far from transparent. This means that subsidies can easily be hidden. This makes countervail cases impossible to prove and it complicates the determination of countervailing duties.

Both Russia and China make extensive use of state trading agencies to manage their international trade. In part this reflects the incompatibility of arbitrarily set prices with international prices. It also reflects inherent protectionism. Given the weak WTO rules regarding state trading agencies, admitting China and Russia would open the WTO to significant protectionist pressures and mercantilist approaches to trade (Ceko and Kerr, 2000). The disciplines on state trading agencies should be substantially improved before they are admitted.

As the commercial legal systems in Russia and China fall far short of the standards of those in modern market economies, intellectual property protection will be problematic at best. Given the weakness of the TRIPS, the threat of trade retaliation is unlikely to be effective. China has a large scientific and technical community that is able to practise intellectual property piracy on a large scale. Russia also has a large cadre that is well equipped with human capital (albeit depreciating in value) that has had to learn to adapt to survive. It seems that they would both be well able to engage in, for example, reverse engineering of the products of biotechnology. All this suggests that the TRIPS will need to be strengthened prior to accession.

Given the level of criminal activity in Russia, even the anti-dumping mechanism may be tested. There is no transparency. Activities such as selling below cost may be part of schemes to launder money or move assets outside Russia. These activities may threaten firms in market economies. Dumping will be difficult to prove even with the poor dumping mechanism that currently exists. Of course, such illegal activities are not predatory pricing.

Tariff collection in Russia is corrupt. This may provide opportunities for discriminatory access to markets. Tariff evaluation is likely to be elastic. Invoice pricing may not reflect true cost and transparency is not sufficient for accurate detection.

The freeing of prices has led to markets in transition economies being in disequilibrium over long periods of time. While integration into the international market may assist in the movement to price equilibrium, it may also be destabilizing to international markets. The markets are also heavily monopolized meaning that they do not reflect relative efficiency (Hobbs, Kerr and Gaisford, 1997). As a result, trade will be distorted.

China and Russia are not market economies. Corruption, cronyism, poor legal systems and incomplete markets are probably as difficult for the international system to deal with as direct intervention in prices.

The accession of China and Russia to the WTO needs to be monitored closely. It will also require the strengthening of the WTO. To accomplish this, more agreements will have to be opened for re-negotiation. The accession of China is crucial not only because of the size of the Chinese economy, but because it may set precedents for Russia. Their economies may, however, be quite different by the time Russia accedes. Getting accession right may be important for the long-term development of the WTO.

NOTES

1. It is useful to refer to this broad type of market structure as *monopolistic competition*. It is monopolistic in the sense that there are sufficiently few firms that each retains some price-setting power, but competitive in the sense that entry dissipates profits in the long run. Economists, however, define monopolistic competition more narrowly, applying it only to cases where products are differentiated and the firms compete in prices (that is, each firm takes the price set by its rivals as given).
2. In practice, there is typically a high degree of vertical coordination through contracts between producers of genetically modified inputs and the farms that use them.
3. Since genetic modification cannot be detected even with experience in consumption, it can be seen as a *credence* characteristic (Nelson, 1970).
4   The term 'adverse selection' comes from the literature on insurance and refers to a situation where households that are subject to the greatest inherent risk have a greater incentive to purchase insurance when insurance providers cannot costlessly observe risk and offer a common premium to all households.
5. While the non-GMF market may in practice bear some of the costs of the separation of supply chains and accentuate the price increase for the non-GMF by shifting the $S1$ curve upward, certified non-GMF imports would tend to reduce the magnitude of the price increase.
6. There is some confusion in the economics literature about the definition of predation. Some definitions suggest that it is the practice of pricing to drive out competition even if no selling below cost takes place. Selling more cheaply than competitors without selling below cost, however, means the firm moving

into a market is simply more efficient than local producers. If the market is subsequently monopolized there may be a place for removal of barriers to entry but it is not the place for dumping remedies.

7. For example, given that Poland has a higher tariff on tomato paste than the Czech Republic, Poland may wish to have rules of origin in the Central European Free Trade Agreement (CEFTA) to prevent China from shipping tomato paste to the Czech Republic at the low Czech tariff and then on to Poland tariff free. CEFTA includes Bulgaria, the Czech Republic, Hungary, Poland, Romania, Slovakia and Slovenia.

8. MERCOSUR consists of Argentina, Brazil, Paraguay and Uruguay. Bolivia and Chile are associates.

9. The European Union had widened to encompass 15 members by 1995. The original members of the European Coal and Steel Community of 1951 and the European Economic Community of 1957 were Belgium, France, Germany, Italy, Luxembourg and the Netherlands. Denmark, Ireland and the United Kingdom joined in 1973, Greece joined in 1981, Spain and Portugal joined in 1986, and Austria, Finland and Sweden joined in 1995.

10. Notice that adverse joint effects of trade diversion could be avoided entirely if Country 1 were to reduce its external tariff sufficiently to maintain imports from the rest at their original level.

11. For any one country entering into an RTA, there will be welfare gains in some markets and losses on others. Overall gains for a particular country are more likely the greater the initial trade with the partner (that is, the less scope for trade diversion) and the higher its own initial tariffs (that is, the more scope for trade creation) if other things are equal.

12. When Canada was required to convert its poultry and dairy import quotas to TRQs as a result of the URAA, the United States argued unsuccessfully that it should get tariff-free access to the Canadian market under NAFTA.

13. Norway, Liechtenstein and Iceland, along with Switzerland, are the remaining members of the European Free Trade Area (EFTA). The European Union has Association Agreements with Bulgaria, Cyprus, the Czech Republic, Estonia, Hungary, Latvia, Lithuania, Malta, Poland, Romania, Slovenia and Slovakia. The Association Agreements do provide minimal quantity-constrained access to EU markets for some agricultural products.

5. Trade in the 21st Century

5.1 PROSPECTS FOR THE NEW ROUND OF TRADE NEGOTIATIONS

The integration of agricultural trade into the general WTO commitments regarding international trade is far from complete. The Uruguay Round represented only the first step in the process. Many who work in agriculture may not realize, and be surprised, that integration was agreed on; yet this was one of the major achievements of the Uruguay Round process. There is little doubt that the framers of the Uruguay Round Agreement on Agriculture (URAA) expected it to be a continuing process. They committed to a resumption of negotiations. Thus there was no presumption that the stage reached at the end of the Uruguay Round process would represent a new *status quo*. Those in private industry and government departments who were not dealing directly with trade issues and who thought they had finished with the development of positions, the provision of input into the negotiation process and explanations of the progress of negotiations to their stakeholders will, if they have not done so already, wake up to find themselves engaged in the process once again. Of course, over the six or seven years since the Uruguay Round many changes in personnel have taken place. The new personnel will have to be brought up to speed on the arcane points of *de minimis* calculations and the mysteries of the blue box. When all is said and done, what goes on in Geneva has large economic impacts and being poorly informed carries considerable risks.

It is also important to recognize that the negotiations in Geneva are just the tip of the iceberg in terms of the effort that surrounds trade negotiations. All those who are engaged in agriculture, from farmers to agribusiness executives to ministers of agriculture, will be bombarded with information, asked for their opinions and feel the need to interpret how distant ideas will affect their particular endeavours. Some will choose to ignore the hubbub but they will not remain untouched. Farm organizations will write briefs, bureaucrats will meet to grapple with a thousand queries, academics will organize conferences and write books, journalists will report and comment, vested interests will lobby, and interest groups will protest. Sometimes it may seem that trade negotiations produce more economic activity than the value of the trade that is eventually affected.

Proposing changes to trade regimes has always provoked strong emotions, from the mercantile debates of the 18th century, to the acrimonious wrangling over repeal of the British 'corn laws' in the 19th to hard-fought elections over NAFTA or European integration in the 20th. One should expect nothing different as we enter the 21st century. Changes in trade regimes will lead to winners and losers, at least in the short run. Trade theory predicts overall gains from trade liberalization, but they are too abstract to observe directly and hence the road of the proponents of liberalization is always more difficult than it should be.

The settlement of the larger issue of the degree to which agricultural trade will be liberalized will be a political compromise worked out within the framework provided by the WTO. It is probably impossible to predict the form or shape of such a political compromise until it is actually arrived at. Given that trade negotiations have ever-widening facets, the possible combinations of trade-offs that could constitute a settlement is probably impossible to compute. The WTO only provides a multilateral forum for the play of international politics.

The narrower, but possibly more important, purpose of the WTO is often lost in the larger issues pertaining to the merits of trade liberalization and the speed at which it should take place. The primary purpose of the WTO is to make rules for trade. The purpose of these rules is to reduce the risks for firms that wish to engage in international commerce. The rules of trade limit the scope of action by governments. Governments guard their sovereignty closely. The trick for rule-making bodies like the WTO is to design rules of trade that provide firms with security but only infringe on sovereignty to a politically acceptable degree. There is always room to improve the security provided by the rules.

One conclusion that should suggest itself to readers is that the existing rules of trade do not provide a satisfactory level of security for firms wishing to invest in international commercial ventures in agriculture. For example, the ability of the European Union to select the products to which its export subsidies apply, and to what degree, reduces the ability of firms that will compete with EU exports to plan effectively. It also hampers the

European Unions's own agribusiness firms which are contemplating investments in export processing facilities (Hobbs, 1995). They too must attempt to predict the market for their products over the life of an investment. Agribusinesses exporting beef need better assurances that they will not face harassment by anti-dumping actions every time the international cattle market is depressed. The changing world of agriculture also requires new transparent rules to be put in place. Farmers in Canada need to know, if they plant transgenic crops, whether they can ultimately be sold in the European Union. Firms investing in biotechnology need to know to what degree their intellectual property rights will be protected in foreign markets.

Progress on providing better security for agribusiness firms that wish to engage in international commerce will be the true test of the WTO. It is important that WTO officials keep that uppermost in their minds and do their best to keep the negotiators focused on this aspect of trade agreements. As well, agribusiness leaders in each country need to remind their governments of their interest in more transparent and risk-reducing rules. Even if considerable liberalization is accomplished, it will have little impact if firms wishing to take advantage of new trade opportunities do not have sufficient security to do so.

A great stride towards increased security for firms would result from agreeing to abandon the anti-dumping provisions or, if that is not possible, to have them improved. Governments should not use anti-dumping actions as a means to protect firms from unanticipated increases in imports. The safeguard provisions that provide direct protection against surges are a much better means to reduce short-run adjustment costs than opaque and inconsistent anti-dumping procedures. It is much simpler for firms to monitor imports and prepare for the relatively automatic trade barriers imposed under anti-surge provisions than it is to prepare defences against accusations of dumping. Of course, there will be considerable resistance to the abandonment of anti-dumping. If it must be retained, a clear statement that it is intended to redress international predatory pricing would go a long way to increasing firms' security. It is far easier for a firm to defend itself against charges of monopolization than price discrimination or selling below average total cost – both of which may be normal business practice. Once redressing international predatory pricing is the explicit objective of anti-dumping provisions, then the existing indefensible criteria can easily be dispensed with and more appropriate criteria developed. It is grey areas that cause the greatest difficulties for firms.

Similar arguments can be made for improving access. The GATT tariff-reducing rounds were so successful because the schedules for tariff reductions were laid out over long periods of time. This transparent information provided the basis for planning. The tariff rate quota (TRQ) process should be moved to this type of formal scheduling. Quota access increasing at 10 per cent per year, or even 1 per cent, until all parties can agree that quotas are no longer relevant, would improve transparency – not only for exporters but also domestic producers. Of course, as pointed out in Chapter 3, increasing quota quantities will not increase market access in all cases. Timetables for quota expansion would also reduce the benefits associated with protectionist rent seeking. In the transparent tariff-cutting GATT process, where levels are 'bound' at each level, one does not often find lobbying for tariff increases. Of course, improvements to the transparency of TRQ administration would also reduce risks for firms engaging in international commercial activities.

Product-by-product schedules for the reduction of export and domestic subsidies would also be preferable to the current reductions in aggregate levels of support. Even if the agreed reductions were slower, the value of the increase in transparency might well offset the gains lost from slower reductions.

On the other hand, the sanitary and phyto-sanitary (SPS), technical barriers to trade (TBT) and safeguard provisions appear to be working well, and as intended. They have clear criteria and probably should not be re-opened for negotiation. The safeguard provisions could be opened to provide somewhat increased protection against surges as a trade-off for abandoning anti-dumping – but not for other reasons. They should only be opened to allow adjustments to trigger levels or sunset periods.

The European Union has asked that the SPS be opened up to deal with consumer concerns. Their experience with the beef hormone case has raised their awareness that the WTO has no mechanism to deal with consumer requests for protection. If the hormone case were a one-off problem, then it would not be of particular concern. The European Union could, as it has chosen to do, ignore the ruling of the WTO panel and accept retaliation. This is probably acceptable as a one-off case. The problem is that consumers (and other groups such as environmentalists) are increasingly lobbying their politicians for protection. The United States already has a number of environmentally motivated mechanisms to restrict trade in products such as fish and seafood that are harvested using environmentally unfriendly methods. These have yet to be tested fully at the WTO but it is clear that the organization has no real means to handle the question. Pretending that environmental requests for protection do not exist as a problem for domestic politicians is simply an example of the WTO behaving like an 'ostrich with its head in the sand'. The WTO needs to deal with these fundamental trade issues if for no other reason than to avoid having them dealt with in multinational forums that do not have international commercial relations as their primary purpose (Phillips and Kerr, 2000). Nothing could be worse for firms engaged in international commerce, and if this happened it would cause the WTO to lose credibility with its primary constituency.

As consumers have become richer, they have begun to value additional product attributes which may have more to do with how products are produced than what they impart when they are consumed. Animal welfare is one example. Widespread consumer resistance is, however, most likely to manifest itself in the area of transgenic food products. Politicians in the European Union are already having to deal with widespread and vociferous consumer requests for protection from transgenic food products (Perdikis and Kerr, 1999). The scientific evidence regarding transgenics is far from complete, but even if it were it is unlikely that all consumers would accept it. This is why the SPS is not the appropriate venue for dealing with the problem. The scientific criteria of the SPS does not matter if consumers will not accept them as valid. Trying to force consumer issues on to the SPS agenda would only muddle what is essentially a good agreement. It may be time for the member countries of the WTO to consider a separate agreement to deal with consumer requests for protection (Perdikis and Kerr, 1999).

Probably the most important thing that needs to be accomplished at the current negotiations is to establish some method of dealing with trade in genetically modified foods (GMFs) and other organisms of agronomic interest. A great technological revolution is just beginning in agriculture. While some may wish to put the 'genie back in its bottle', it has in fact already escaped. There is no turning back. It may be possible to regulate the use of the technology in developed countries and to put expensive identity preservation systems in place to separate transgenic from non-transgenic products. Even if this is possible, it is likely to lead to a plethora of trade disputes and even more ongoing animosity among developed countries over agricultural trade. The real problem, however, will be in developing countries where regulatory capacity is limited. Crops will be produced using transgenic technology in developing countries – there is no way to stop it. If complicated regulatory regimes to control the imports of transgenics are mandated by developed countries and given approval at the WTO, developing countries may simply not be able to meet them. This would mean disruption to all of their exports where transgenic products exist – one bad apple spoiling the lot. This could have serious ramifications for their short-run economic stability and long-run development. Thus, getting a regulatory regime for GMFs in place will be of central importance at the new round of negotiations.

It is probably unfortunate that most of the rhetoric and wrangling that will go on at the new round of negotiations – negotiations to start a new millennium – will relate to yesterday's issues – export subsidy reductions, domestic levels of support for farmers, market access. The compromises that are eventually reached on these 'old' issues will simply be political – even if the arguments are dressed up in economic jargon. This does not mean that what eventually emerges will not have significant economic ramifications for firms that wish to engage in international commerce and for the member states of the WTO. There are, however, a large number of new and vitally important issues that require inventive solutions. They should command the lion's share of the human capital that is expended on trade negotiations. Unfortunately, this is unlikely to be the case.

5.2 THE FUTURE OF AGRICULTURAL TRADE

Agricultural trade will continue to be a growth industry no matter what is decided – or not decided – at agricultural trade negotiations. Global demographic trends dictate that conclusion. Population growth will be rapid for the first quarter of the 21st century and will, at best, only slow thereafter. Food consumption peaks after population as individuals reach adulthood. Most of the population growth will occur in developing countries. The food requirements of the developing world's additional population will be met largely by squeezing more out of its already taxed resources. New technology will help in increasing output but in the end it will not be enough. Some food – and by this we mean very large quantities – will have to come from exporting countries in the developed world. Their domestic food consumption will be flat at best and there will be additional potential production capacity available. The new technologies that will help increase food production in developing countries will help developed countries' farmers even more.

While the world's net agricultural exporting countries will, in the short run, continue to focus on the forgone opportunities which the largely unattainable EU market represents, over time their attention will be drawn more and more to markets in developing countries. With any expansion of export subsidies largely controlled, there should be relatively free competition for these expanding markets. This does not mean that competition for the growing markets will not be fierce. It will be.

It is sometimes argued that, while there will be a need for more food in developing countries, there will be no money to pay for it. This is largely a myth. Development is taking place. With some notable exceptions, developing countries have finally set aside many of the inappropriate policies which were put in place in the 1950s, 1960s and 1970s when they were attempting to develop through import substitution. Certainly, not all people in developing countries will share in the benefits of development. However, most will, and they will use a considerable proportion of their new income on more and then better food. There will still be countries where agriculture fails due to war, ecological mismanagement or bad weather. Some of these countries will not be able to pay for food and will be candidates for food aid. They will be exceptions, not the rule.

The WTO has consistently given developing countries special treatment in agricultural trade. This does not seem wise. The arguments that support trade liberalization are equally valid for all countries. The benefits that arise from trade liberalization may be even more important for developing countries than they are for developed countries. Trade restrictions mean that economic opportunities are forgone. To develop, there is a need to remove constraints on efficiency and other sources of economic opportunity. Thus, allowing developing countries to keep trade barriers and trade-distorting subsidies at levels that exceed those of developed countries may be an important constraint on their development. Allowing least developed countries to do nothing towards trade liberalization may be particularly divisive.

Developing countries will, however, be faced with higher adjustment costs. Poorly educated labour will have a difficult time moving into growth sectors. In certain circumstances some intervention to slow adjustment may be justified (Leger, Gaisford and Kerr, 1999). Trade measures, however, are seldom the most efficient mechanism to mitigate the costs of adjustment. On a practical level, to account for this relative adjustment cost problem, developing and least developed countries should have to keep to the same standards as developed countries but be allowed longer phase-in periods or slower sunsets. Allowing developing and least developed countries to violate the central non-discrimination tenet of the WTO has been a major failing of the member states collectively.

Protectionists in developing countries have become masters in the art of trotting out all of the tired protectionist arguments, often dressed up in new clothes. They are no more compelling now than they were 150 years ago when they were used to justify the development of Germany, 100 years ago to justify the development of central Europe or 50 years ago to justify the development of Latin America. When developing countries have largely abandoned protectionism to develop industry, it seems a great inconsistency to continue to apply it to agriculture. Of course, developed countries are no strangers to this inconsistency.

The opening of developing countries' agricultural markets will let the sector make a real contribution to the development process. It will also allow the growing demand for food to be effectively managed, and free up government resources to deal with real cases of need.

Other forces are at work that will break down the protectionism that exists in developed countries. The European Union is set to expand eastward. Some expansion to include selected countries in central Europe would likely have already taken place if it were not for the Common Agricultural Policy (CAP). The central problem for the European Union is how to take in new members without having to extend them the benefits of the CAP. Even if the short-run costs would be acceptable to EU taxpayers, the European Union's high price regimes would provide incentives for re-investment and entry in the acceding countries that would make the CAP, at least as currently financed, fiscally untenable. Schemes for entry without the inclusion of agriculture or only partial extensions of the CAP are ultimately inconsistent with a common market and doomed to failure. The European Union may ultimately decide not to expand. This will force the countries of central and eastern Europe to re-focus on world markets instead of on the distorted prices in the European Union. The dashed expectations that would accompany this course of action will lead to long-term hostility towards the European Union that will show up in a wide range of venues, including the WTO. This will make it more difficult for the European Union to defend its agricultural trade policies and force more long-run trade-offs in future broad-based WTO negotiations.

If eastward expansion does takes place, it will, either before or after the event, force a restructuring of the CAP. Trade barriers and trade-distorting subsidies will come down and the full integration of agriculture into general WTO disciplines will be hastened.

Even Japan is finding it increasingly difficult to defend its protectionist policies towards agriculture. When the Japanese economy was experiencing consistently rapid rates of growth, it was easy to force consumers to share part of their increasing incomes with farmers though high prices and to tax growing urban incomes to provide subsidies. The Japanese economy has ceased to grow at rates experienced in the past. Realization that the Japanese economy has fundamentally changed has been slow to sink in (Cruz and Kerr, 2000). At first, the economic malaise was perceived as an anomaly or possibly as part of a cycle. This is the same trap other developed countries fell into during the 1970s and 1980s. Following 25 years of sustained and rapid growth, after the mid-1970s, if there was growth at all, it was at much lower rates. Developed countries thought previous levels of growth would return. At first they borrowed to pay for the social programmes which had been put in place on the expectation of continued high rates of growth. After more than a decade, it began to sink in that growth was not going to return to previous levels and that the tax base would not automatically expand to cover the increasing cost of social programmes.

Hard choices were then made. Budget deficits were reined in through varying combinations of expenditure restraint, tax increases and waste reduction. Japan has not yet reached this stage; it is still waiting for the 'good times' to return, but after a decade that expectation is wearing a little thin. If growth does not return soon, Japan will have to begin looking at reforms. With much smaller general social programmes than other developed countries, there will be less to cut. Agriculture is an exception. Consumers and taxpayers will begin to question the country's high-price, high-expenditure agricultural policy. This will force the government to examine its agricultural trade policy closely. It will also need trade concessions from its trading partners as it tries to re-vitalize its industrial sector. It will have to have something to offer in exchange.

The long-run prospects for agricultural trade are, hence, very positive. While the hog farmer in Iowa or the Saskatchewan grain farmer who is struggling to make ends meet in depressed markets will find little solace in these long-term prospects, trade policy actually has little to do with their problems.

Trade policy cannot correct the difficulties caused by the long-term process of technical change in agriculture. If the European Union had never had the CAP and Japan had been willing right from the start to let its citizens eat imported rice and beef, the forces of technological change would have led to much more rapid rationalization of their agriculture. The majority of European and Japanese land would still be in production, but their farmers would be much more efficient. Technological change would still be putting farmers on the increased productivity, lower prices treadmill that they have been on for more than a century.

If countries had never put up trade barriers in the first place, however, the firms that wish to engage in international commercial relations in agriculture would have been faced with much lower levels of risk. Their investments in trade activities would have been commensurately higher. Trade levels would be higher and probably the conduct of trade more efficient.

International trade agreements and the institutions put in place to administer them, such as the WTO, cannot solve agricultural problems. The use of trade measures can, at best, lead to short-run gains for some vested interests. Given that, over the long run, the benefits of trade policy will be capitalized, it is the owners of fixed assets who are the prime beneficiaries. None of this is new. It is the stuff of undergraduate courses in agricultural economics.

Intervention in international markets by governments is not, however, neutral. It reduces transparency and increases risks for those who wish to engage in international commerce. This side effect of trade policy exacerbates inefficiencies. Whatever their stance on protection, the member countries of the WTO should work to reduce such side effects. The WTO, as an organization, should try to steer member countries away from creating or retaining inefficiencies. The WTO is only a forum where the political wrangling over agricultural protectionism takes place, not the arbitrator of that process nor the guardian of trade liberalization. The WTO is, however, the repository of the rules of trade and their arbitrator. If the latter role is done well, the agricultural trade of the future will be conducted with much less difficulty than in the past.

References

Akerlof, G.A. (1970), 'The Market for Lemons: Quality Uncertainty and the Market Mechanism', *Quarterly Journal of Economics*, **84**, 488–500.

Braga, C.A.P. (1995), 'Trade-related Intellectual Property Issues: The Uruguay Round Agreement and Its Economic Implications', in W. Martin and L.A. Winters (eds), *The Uruguay Round and the Developing Economies*, World Bank Discussion Paper No. 307, World Bank, Washington, D.C., pp. 381–411.

Caswell, J.A. and N. Hooker (1996), 'HACCP as an International Trade Standard', *American Journal of Agricultural Economics*, **78** (3), 775–9.

Ceko, T. and W.A. Kerr (2000), *Accommodating a Square Peg: China's Accession to the WTO*, EPRI Report No. 00-01, Excellence in the Pacific Research Institute, University of Lethbridge, Lethbridge.

Cruz, H.A. and W.A. Kerr (2000), *Long Solar Eclipse or Setting Sun? The Japanese Economy and Globalisation*, EPRI Report No. 00-02, Excellence in the Pacific Research Institute, University of Lethbridge Lethbridge.

European Commission (1997), *The Agricultural Situation in the European Union, 1997 Report*, European Commission Brussels.

FAPRI (Food and Agricultural Policy Research Institute) (1998), *FAPRI 1998 World Agricultural Outlook*, Iowa State University and University of Missouri-Columbia, Ames and Columbia.

Gaisford, J.D. and C.H. Lau (2000), 'The Case for and against Import Embargoes on Products of Biotechnology', *The Estey Centre Journal of International Law and Trade Policy*, **1** (1), 83–98, http://www.esteyjournal.com.

Gaisford, J.D. and R.S. Richardson (1994), *North–South Disputes over the Protection of Intellectual Property*, Discussion Paper No. 94-03, Department of Economics, University of Calgary, Calgary.

187

GATT (General Agreement on Tariffs and Trade) (1993), *Focus: GATT Newsletter*, No. 104 (December).

Gillis, K.G., W.A. Kerr, C.D. White, S.M. Ulmer and A.S. Kwaczec (1985), 'The Prospects for Export of Primal Beef Cuts to California', *Canadian Journal of Agricultural Economics*, **33** (2), 171–94.

Gordon, D.V., R. Hannesson and W.A. Kerr (2000), 'Of Fish and Whales: The Credibility of Threats in International Trade Disputes', *Journal of Policy Modeling* (forthcoming).

Hadfield, G.K. and D. Thomson (1998), 'An Information based Approach to Labeling Biotechnology Consumer Products', *Journal of Consumer Policy*, **21**, 551–78.

Hemnes, T.M.S., M.G. DiMambro and M.L. Moore (1992), *Intellectual Property World Desk Reference*, Kluwer Law and Taxation Publishers Deventer, The Netherlands.

Henderson, R.D. and W.A. Kerr (1984/85), 'The Theory and Practice of Economic Relations between CMEA Member States and African Countries', *Journal of Contemporary African Studies*, **4** (1–2), 3–35.

Hertel, T.W., M. Brockmeier and P.V. Swaminathan (1997), 'Sectoral and Economy-wide Analysis of Integrating Central and Eastern European Countries into the EU: Implications of Alternative Strategies', *European Review of Agricultural Economics* **24**, 359–86.

Hobbs, J. E. (1995), 'Evolving Marketing Channels for Beef and Lamb in the United Kingdom – A Transaction Cost Approach', *Journal of International Food and Agribusiness Marketing*, **7** (4), 15–35.

Hobbs, J.E., W.A. Kerr and J.D. Gaisford (1997), *The Transformation of the Agrifood Sectors of Central and Eastern Europe and the New Independent States*, CAB International, Wallingford.

Hobbs, J.E. and M.D. Plunkett (1999), 'Genetically Modified Foods: Consumer Issues and the Role of Information Asymmetry', *Canadian Journal of Agricultural Economics* (forthcoming).

Kerr, W.A. (1988), 'The Canada–United States Free Trade Agreement and the Livestock Sector: The Second Stage Negotiations', *Canadian Journal of Agricultural Economics*, **36** (4), 895–903.

Kerr, W.A. (1997), 'Removing Health, Sanitary and Technical Non-tariff Barriers in NAFTA – A New Institutional Economics Paradigm', *Journal of World Trade*, **31** (5), 57–73.

Kerr, W.A. (1999), 'International Trade in Transgenic Food Products: A New Focus for Agricultural Trade Disputes', *World Economy*, **22** (2), 245–59.

Kerr, W.A. (2000), *WTO and the Environment*, Paper presented at a symposium entitled 'Globalisation and New Agricultural Trade Rules for the 21st Century', Saskatoon, Saskatchewan, 12–14 February.

Kerr, W.A., J.E. Hobbs and R. Yampoin (1999), 'Intellectual Property Protection, Biotechnology and Developing Countries; Will the TRIPS Be Effective?', *AgBioForum*, **2** (3–4), 203–11.

Kerr, W.A., K.K. Klein, J.E. Hobbs and M. Kagatsume (1994), *Marketing Beef in Japan*, Haworth, New York.

Kerr, W.A. and E. MacKay (1997) 'Is Mainland China Evolving into a Market Economy?', *Issues and Studies*, **33** (9), 31–45.

Kerr, W.A. and N. Perdikis (1995), *The Economics of International Business*, Chapman & Hall London.

Koulen, M. (1995), 'The New Anti-dumping Code through Its Negotiating History', in J.H.J. Bourreois, F. Berrod and E.G. Fournier (eds), *The Uruguay Round Results: A European Lawyers' Perspective*, European Interuniversity Press, Brussels, pp. 151–246.

Leger, L.A., J.D. Gaisford and W.A. Kerr (1999) 'Labour Market Adjustments to International Trade Shocks', in S.B. Dahiya (ed.), *The Current State of Economic Science*, Spellbound Publishers, Rohtak, pp 2011–34.

McGee, J.S. (1958), 'Predatory Price Cutting in the Standard Oil (N.J.) Case', *Journal of Law and Economics*, **1**, 137–69.

Mooney, S. and K.K. Klein (1999), 'Environmental Concerns and Risks of Genetically Modified Crops: Economic Contributions to the Debate', *Canadian Journal of Agricultural Economics* (forthcoming).

Morris, P. and K. Anderson (1999), *Redefining Agriculture in the WTO: Creating One Class of Goods*, Center for Trade Policy Studies Conference, Seattle, November.

Nelson, P. (1970), 'Information and Consumer Behaviour', *Journal of Political Economy*, **78**, 311–29.

OECD (Organization for Economic Cooperation and Development) (1998), *Agricultural Policies in OECD Countries: Measurement of Support and Background Information*, OECD, Paris.

OECD (Organization for Economic Cooperation and Development) (1999), *Agricultural Policies in OECD Countries: Monitoring and Evaluation*, OECD, Paris.

Perdikis, N. and W.A. Kerr (1998), *Trade Theories and Empirical Evidence* Manchester University Press, Manchester.

Perdikis, N. and W.A. Kerr (1999), 'Can Consumer based Demands for Protection Be Incorporated in the WTO? The Case of Genetically Modified Foods', *Canadian Journal of Agricultural Economics* (forthcoming).

Perdikis, N., W.A. Kerr and J.E. Hobbs (1999), *Can the WTO/GATT Agreements on Phyto-Sanitary Measures and Technical Barriers to Trade Be Renegotiated to Accommodate Agricultural Biotechnology?*, Paper presented at a conference entitled 'Transitions in Agbiotech: Economics of Strategy and Policy', NE-165, Washington, D.C., June.

Phillips, P.W.B. and W.A. Kerr (2000), *The BioSafety Protocol and International Trade in Genetically Modified Organisms*, CATRN Paper No. 2000-03, Canadian Agrifood Trade Research Network, http://www.eru.ulaval.ca.catrn/ .

Plunkett, M.D. and J.D. Gaisford (2000), 'Limiting Biotechnology? Information Problems and Policy Reponses', *Current Agriculture and Resource Issues: An Economic Journal* (forthcoming).

Podbury, T. and I. Roberts (1999), *WTO Agricultural Negotiations: Important Market Access Issues*, ABARE Research Report No. 99.3, Australian Bureau of Agricultural and Resource Economics, Canberra.

Roberts, D. (1998), 'Preliminary Assessment of the Effects of the WTO Agreement on Sanitary and Phytosanitary Regulations', *Journal of International Economics Law*, 377–405.

Schieb, P.A. (1999), 'Feeding Tomorrow's World', *OECD Observer*, Nos. 217/218, pp. 37–40.

Schmitz, A., R.S. Firch and J.S. Hillman (1981), 'Agricultural Export Dumping: The Case of Mexican Winter Vegetables in the U.S. Market', *American Journal of Agricultural Economics*, **63** (4), 645–54.

Sherwood, R.M. (1990), *Intellectual Property and Economic Development*, Westview Press, Boulder.

Skully, D.W. (1999), *The Economics of TRQ Administration*, IATRC Working Paper No. 99-6, International Agricultural Trade Research Consortium, Washington, D.C.

Stanton, G.H. (1995), 'Understanding the GATT Agreement on the Application of Sanitary and Phytosanitary Measures', *Food, Nutrition and Agriculture*, **11**, 36–42.

Swinbank, A. (1999), 'EU Agriculture, Agenda 2000 and the WTO Commitments', *World Economy*, **22** (1), 41–54.

Tarvydas, R., J.D. Gaisford, J.E. Hobbs and W.A. Kerr (1999), *Agricultural Biotechnology in Developing Countries – Market-based Technology Transfer or Piracy?* presented at a conference entitled 'Transitions in Agbiotech: Economics of Stategy and Policy', NE-165, Washington D.C., June.

Tharakan, P.K.M. (1999), 'Is Anti-dumping Here to Stay?', *World Economy*, **22** (2), 179–206.

WTO (World Trade Organization) (1999), Website, http://www.wto.org/ (October 10).

Yampoin, R. and W.A. Kerr (1998) 'Can Trade Measures Induce Compliance with TRIPS?', *Journal of the Asia Pacific Economy*, **3** (2), 165–82.

Yeung, M.T., N. Perdikis and W.A. Kerr (1999), *Regional Trading Blocs in the Global Economy – The EU and ASEAN*, Edward Elgar, Cheltenham.

Zampetti, A.B. (1995), 'The Uruguay Round Agreement on Subsidies – A Forward Looking Assessment', *Journal of World Trade*, **29** (6), 5–29.

Index